Praise for

THE UNFAIR ADVANTAGE

"Compelling, powerful and engaging! Dr. Harold Arnold has woven prayerful inspiration and direction into a powerful recipe for reaping the richness and joy God intended for marriage. *The Unfair Advantage* is a message for anyone who wants to unwrap the promises of one of God's greatest gifts."

—Jim Akers
Author of *Tape Breakers*

"I thoroughly enjoyed reading and learning from this precious book. I will be rereading it many times and will use it to counsel others in the path to a godly marriage. Well done, Dr. Arnold!"

—H. Guthrie Chamberlain
Founder, The Christian Podcasting Network

"Dr. Arnold sheds new light on marriage via an unexpected passage in Scripture. At first glance, it has nothing to do with marriage. After much consideration, and with Dr. Arnold's encouragement, it becomes apparent—it has everything to do with marriage. If you take Dr. Arnold's insight, advice and encouragement to heart, you will embark on a journey to a more meaningful personal faith and a more rewarding, productive marriage."

—Rick Coplin
Host of *The Success to Significance* podcast

"Dr. Harold Arnold has uniquely and biblically simplified the union of marriage. As a stepmother myself, I transparently profess the fundamental importance of building a blended family on a biblically-based marriage. Dr. Arnold's book will be a prerequisite within my coaching and mentoring business."

—Stephanie Lefler
CEO, Mom University

"In *The Unfair Advantage*, Dr. Harold Arnold provides a clear God-centered path that will not only strengthen your union, but will help remind you that marriage is truly one of God's greatest gifts."

—Denise LaRosa
CEO Mom Talk with Denise LaRosa LLC
Author of *Empty Shoes*

"In *The Unfair Advantage*, Dr. Harold Arnold shares clear systems and processes for being as intentional about success in your marriage as you would in business. He draws deeply on biblical Scripture for principles that assure us that 'if you practice these qualities you will never fail.' And today, with a thriving marriage, those around you will indeed assume you have an 'unfair advantage.'"

—Dan Miller
New York Times best-selling author and coach (48Days.com)

"In *The Unfair Advantage*, Dr. Harold Arnold, Jr. does a masterful job at laying out seven principles we can use to build a thriving, healthy and successful marriage. He understands the complexities of marriage and the various elements, both natural and spiritual, that can undermine a healthy one. His practical steps, grounded in Scripture, make this book a must-read for any couple struggling in a marriage that seems hopeless or lost."

—David Mooring, MBA
President/CEO of BurlapSky, Inc.

“Many of us have fallen for the accusatory lie of our enemy: ‘You will never have the marriage God wants you to have!’ Dr. Arnold shares that, while it is true that ‘marriage is spiritual warfare with relational consequences,’ we have an unfair advantage. Dr. Arnold has not written another marriage handbook; he has woven a practical theology from the ‘7 grace habits’ of 2 Peter 1:3–11 with practical applications that will empower couples to experience a godly marriage.”

—Dr. Bruce McCracken
Founder and President of House on the Rock Family Ministries

“Initially I reacted to the title, *The Unfair Advantage*, probably like some of you. I wondered, ‘How could a Christian marriage have an unfair advantage?’ Knowing Dr. Harold Arnold as I do, I realized that somewhere along the way he would provide a brilliant spiritual twist on the phrase ‘unfair advantage’ to show the magnificent role grace plays to enable Christian marriages to win. I was right!”

—Dr. Johnny Parker
Turn the Page Leadership Consultant, Executive Coach
Former Chaplain of the Washington Redskins

“With personal stories and Scriptures, Dr. Arnold describes the ‘unfair advantage’ that takes couples from warring to winning. This book is written for those who want to dive deeper into the real reason why God put you together. The wisdom gleaned from this book will reveal godly reasons to stay married—and make your soul happy. Another win for the home team!”

—Pam Perry
PR coach, PamPerryPR.com

"*The Unfair Advantage* is one of those rare books that meticulously unpacks the often overlooked nexus between faith, grace and marital success. Dr. Arnold takes the time to carpool us through a colorful and vivid journey toward spiritual and relational maturity along the highway of 2 Peter 1:3–11. This trip will most certainly awaken your soul, while providing you with a framework for understanding God's plan for making unfairness your advantage. Enjoy the ride!"

—Gene Redd, J.D.
CEO, The Marriage Mentoring Network
Author of *Inside the Mind of a Godly Husband*

"Dr. Harold Arnold, Jr. undergirds every chapter with Scriptural support, illustrated by personal and anecdotal stories that make the teaching come alive. I recommend this book not only to you who are struggling in a marriage, but also to you who want a stronger, more fulfilling marriage."

—Harold J. Sala, Ph.D.
Founder of Guidelines International
Author of *The Parent Map*

"You don't want to just survive in your marriage. You want to thrive. And you need tools to do that. *The Unfair Advantage* brings a different message and a different perspective on how to thrive in your marriage. This book is not just a resource on what to do. It tells you the reason and the power behind doing it. It is a must-read for soon-to-be married and married couples regardless of the stage of marriage."

—Christine K. St. Vil
Founder/CEO, Moms 'N Charge

THE UNFAIR ADVANTAGE

THE UNFAIR ADVANTAGE

A GRACE-INSPIRED PATH TO WINNING AT MARRIAGE

Dr. Harold L. Arnold, Jr.

CLC
PUBLICATIONS
Fort Washington, PA 19034

The Unfair Advantage
Published by CLC Publications

U.S.A.
P.O. Box 1449, Fort Washington, PA 19034

UNITED KINGDOM
CLC International (UK)
Unit 5, Glendale Avenue, Sandycroft, Flintshire, CH5 2QP

Published 2016

Printed in the United States of America.

ISBN (paperback): 978-1-61958-232-3
ISBN (e-book): 978-1-61958-233-0

Italics in Scripture quotations are the emphasis of the author.

Dedication

This book is dedicated to a beautiful young man, Johnny "Tre" Wyche III, whose untimely death at the tender age of twenty-one inspires me to take nothing for granted and live life to the fullest.

Contents

Acknowledgments

This book could not exist except for a single truth: I am married to an exceptional woman, Dalia Ward Arnold, who has loved me even when she did not like me. She trusted God to bring her joy when I struggled to give her that which she deserved. She remains committed to a godly marriage even when the visible signs betray her. She believes in me, possibly more than I deserve. I am so thankful to her for being my unfair advantage and helping me strive for an extraordinary faith.

Prologue

When I was approached with the idea of writing another book on marriage, I deeply considered whether I really had something unique to say that has not been written among the thousands of already-published marriage books—including my own previous two. Frankly, I was not enthused about rehashing or repackaging well-used anecdotes, communication techniques, conflict-resolution skills, and cliché Scriptures that are far too common among secular and faith-based marriage resources. I do not say this to disparage any existing books. I simply want to point out that if this is the type of book you seek, there are many other books from which you can choose. This is not *that* book.

I sought God with one simple request: "Father, if it is Your will for me to write another book on marriage—a book that promises to *touch the heart* of Your people—please show me a clear message." With an already full schedule, I only wanted to sacrifice the time and energy to write a book that was unquestionably guided by the Holy Spirit to touch people's hearts. With my petition before the Lord, I waited for His guidance. As commonly happens, however, the Lord's response did not come as I expected. His answer came to me in three discrete stages.

Within a relatively short period of time, the Lord gave me the book's main title, *The Unfair Advantage*. Although I knew this was confirmation that the Holy Spirit was indeed nudging me to write this book, I thought the title was odd for a marriage book. I thought to myself, "What exactly does 'unfair advantage' have to do with marriage?" Wanting a scriptural basis to clarify the Lord's intent, I again waited for God's answer.

In time, the Holy Spirit led me to a somewhat familiar chapter, Second Peter 1, as the book's scriptural source. The first time I read this chapter, I thought, "What does this have to do with marriage?" So I read it again and again; and with each reading, my excitement grew as the marriage connection crystallized.

I have read many marriage books, and written some too. Over the years, I've also conducted counseling sessions and seminars with thousands of couples. It's truly a privilege to be among a community of Christian marriage educators. Yet, with all of my experiences in this marriage vineyard, never before had I heard such a nuanced synthesis of faith and marriage as the Holy Spirit unveiled during the writing of this book.

As my days of writing turned into weeks and months, I gained increased clarity into why so many Christian marriages fail to reach God's promise for them. I realized that the Lord had directed me to a passage not typically associated with marriage to convey a cardinal truth—that marriage's ultimate promise lay in wholeheartedly living an authentic God-centered faith.

With this enriched understanding of faith and marriage, the Holy Spirit positioned me for the final unveiling. In fact, you probably noticed it in this book's subtitle, *A Grace-Inspired Path to Winning at Marriage.*

Indeed, faith and marriage are fraught with disappointments and hurts. It is only through a grace-laden lens that we'll see a marriage ever reach its promise because, as the apostle Paul so eloquently captures in Romans 3:23, "For all have sinned and fall short of the glory of God."

I began writing this book with a simple request to God—to give me a message that would touch the heart of His people. I believe the Father's response is captured in these pages; but just putting words on paper was never my ultimate goal. My prayer is more personal. I pray that you will see how your own personal struggles and victories give you the inalienable right to lay claim to your unfair advantage. With faith and grace as your guides, I believe the Holy Spirit will seal His promises in your heart.

The Unfair Advantage's Key Scripture Verse

> His divine power has granted to us all things that pertain to life and godliness, through the knowledge of him who called us to his own glory and excellence, by which he has granted to us his precious and very great promises, so that through them you may become partakers of the divine nature, having escaped from the corruption that is in the world because of sinful desire. For this very reason, make every effort to supplement your faith with virtue, and virtue with knowledge, and knowledge with self-control, and self-control with steadfastness, and steadfastness with godliness, and godliness with brotherly affection, and brotherly affection with love. For if these qualities are yours and are increasing, they keep you from being ineffective or unfruitful in the knowledge of our Lord Jesus Christ. For whoever lacks these qualities is so nearsighted that he is blind, having forgotten that he was cleansed from his former sins. Therefore, brothers, be all the

more diligent to confirm your calling and election, for if you practice these qualities you will never fall. For in this way there will be richly provided for you an entrance into the eternal kingdom of our Lord and Savior Jesus Christ. (2 Pet. 1:3–11)

Part 1: A Marriage Mindset

1

A Tale of Two Marriages

Sometimes you don't realize your own strength until you come face to face with your greatest weakness.

—Susan Gale

More than twenty-seven years ago, I stood tall at the altar confidently staring at the beautiful young woman to whom I was about to pledge my life. When I'm most honest, I can admit that I had little idea what I was actually doing. Oh sure . . . in front of family and friends, I was full of bravado that my mother was wrong in her claim that at twenty-two years of age I was too young to marry. "It is not about age but faith," I thought. My fiancé, Dalia, and I were a young Christian couple who felt quite secure in our faith. Yes, our faith *then* felt unshakable. We believed that God had brought us together for a purpose. We felt secure that our love for God— and one another—would empower us to stay monogamously faithful to one another for a lifetime. We were convinced that our Christian convictions would sustain us through the ups and downs of what we knew, even at our young ages, was a covenant relationship.

The ceremony had its flaws; but inside the small brick church in southern New Jersey, among extended family, college friends and well-wishers, we exchanged loving smiles, the best rings our meager budgets could afford and solemn vows. After the lighting of our unity candle and the requisite kiss of the bride, the pastor officially pronounced us husband and wife as licensed by the State of New Jersey. By all accounts, it was a joyous day, full of promise for young Christian lovers who were full of faith—or so we thought.

In Eden, to be married was to experience God.
But then sin happened.

Trouble in Paradise

It didn't take long for trouble to brew. Dogged by differences in personality, life priorities, marital presumptions and the assumptions of our extended families, we seemed to face one minor conflict after another. Sometimes silly things morphed into significant confrontations. "Why didn't you make up the bed since you were the last one in it?" sounded harsher from my mouth than it should have. "Why are you on the computer all the time?" Dalia questioned in a slightly too condescending tone.

I'm not suggesting that things were all bad. We definitely had good times too. Many of our struggles were the typical adjustments that couples make for harmonious living. One thing was for sure—the marriage we'd imagined was *not* the marriage we were living, and that took a toll. Dalia would later reveal that our first year of marriage was the worst year of her life. "I don't deserve this," she told me. For Dalia, marriage felt unfair—a far cry from the dream she'd embraced.

Admittedly, I was less frustrated than Dalia, largely because my dominant personality style usually resulted in me getting more of what I wanted and leaving her holding the proverbial "short end of the stick." Dalia admits that she wasn't blameless either, as her unbridled emotions often ignited firestorms intended to burn me.

Sometimes she'd upset me so much that I'd try to manipulate the situation by emotionally shutting down. In fact, weeks went by when I literally refused to even speak a single word to her—until I ultimately spoke the piercing words, "We are not a team." Even as I'd listen to her sobs in an adjacent room, my calloused heart refused to empathize. It's no wonder that Dalia eventually admitted to me, "Harold, I love you, but I don't like you."

I was stunned. This was one of those moments when both air and words escaped me. I felt like I had received an unfair, ego-bruising punch below the belt. My analytical mind frantically raced with sobering questions. What happened to that young Christian couple so full of faith and love? How could we have fallen so far, so fast from such a promising start? Had my mother's caution that we were just too young to marry been right all along?

Repeat Offenders

It is humbling to reflect on those early years of marriage. Yes, Dalia and I had many admirable qualities, including a staunch refusal to abandon our marriage. Looking back, however, one thing is unequivocally clear: we were both disobedient and dishonoring to the covenant with God to spend our lifetime serving one another. "Disobedient and dishonoring" may seem a harsh critique, but a close look at Scripture's admonition in Ephesians 5:33 succinctly posits the standard to which God holds our marriage: "Let each one of you love his wife as himself, and let the wife see that she respects her husband." We, beyond a shadow of a doubt, behaved as if our marriage belonged to us rather than to God, whom we had committed it to just a short time ago. Like the unrepentant felon who returns to his criminal ways upon release from incarceration, we too were repeat offenders, frequently exchanging barbs of disrespect and disapproval to manipulate situations in our own favor.

We quickly forget that our spouse is not our problem.

God designed marriage to be a garden full of sensuous beauty, much like the garden of Eden where the first marriage was consummated. Even amid the beauty of Eden, and having created Adam as His masterpiece, God deemed it "not good" that Adam should be alone (Gen. 2:18). God responds by creating a "helper," which transliterated from the Hebrew word *neged* means "counterpart." Only when Adam (part) and Eve (counterpart) are united does God introduce the one-flesh relationship, symbolizing what would become His bridegroom-bride relationship with the church. In Eden, to be married was to experience God. But then sin happened.

Through interactions with hundreds of couples since my early years of marriage, I now know that Dalia and I were not the only repeat offenders guilty of disobedience to this godly covenant. Since Adam and Eve's disobedience to God, the institution that was designed to be like a garden has devolved into an active battleground for a war of attrition. The evidence of this struggle surrounds us.

Our culture is littered with an alarming number of marriages in some state of legal, emotional and spiritual dissolution. In a *Woman's Day* survey of 35,000 married women, 72 percent have considered leaving their husbands, and more than half have admitted that they sometimes regret marrying at all.[1]

I recently appeared on *Marriage Beyond the Vows*, a weekly Christian radio call-in program based out of Philadelphia.[2] I was surprised to hear that many husbands are convinced that their wives deliberately withhold physical intimacy. These husbands believe that their wives, in a perverted effort to keep their own Christian consciences clear, hope to manipulate them to file for divorce.

Culture is awash with Christian couples who feel emotionally abused and are teetering on the verge of collapse under a barrage of minor to major repeat offenses. Even an untrained eye can see the frayed fabric of traditional marriage, where the odds of divorce among Christians are about fifty-fifty and where even marriages that survive are failing to thrive.

Many spouses immediately "get it" when their marriage is compared to a battle, but who exactly are the combatants in this eternal conflict?

Although you might believe that your husband or your wife is to blame, they are not—and neither are you. So, what is happening to our Christian marriages?

Collateral Damage

Whether addressing communication challenges, trust deficits, financial woes, intimacy lapses or other marriage maladies, the root issue is not a human one at all. The truth is that since the first covenant relationship between Adam and Eve, marriage has been a spiritual battle between God and Satan. Let's think of it this way—marriage is a spiritual battle with relational consequences.

Jesus gives powerful imagery of Satan's "take no prisoners" approach to spiritual warfare when He tells Simon Peter of Satan's desire to sift him like wheat (see Luke 22:31). In our nonagrarian culture today, we often underestimate the violence in the sifting imagery Jesus offers. Sifting wheat is a violent action, separating the grain (wheat berry) from the stalk and the chaff. Through this metaphor, Jesus clearly conveys Satan's singular objective against us as spiritual separation from God with all of the collateral damage that it implies.

Like a domino reaction, Satan knows that if he separates you from your spiritual source, your Christian marriage will fall in time too. Satan wants to manipulate husbands and wives as expendable pawns in his battle for the hearts and minds of our culture. But, like a magician deftly using misdirection to sell the trick, Satan's insidious strategy hinges on keeping couples distracted from his true intentions.

How long can Satan keep husbands and wives blaming one another for their unhappiness? How deeply can he mire each spouse in self-centered pursuits? What must he do to encourage Christian couples to depend on their own strength rather than draw from God's supply? From my own firsthand experience, my message to you is that Satan is a master of distraction, a nefarious illusionist bent on your individual and mutual destruction.

As he successfully did with Dalia and me for too long, Satan plants seeds of discord that first manifest themselves as little seedlings (minor conflicts), but grow like wild weeds (major conflicts) that threaten to separate us from everything we hold dear. When embroiled in our emotionally taxing daily struggles, we quickly forget that our spouse is not our problem. If we fail to see these challenges as opportunities to mature our faith, our marriage suffers. With blatant disregard for fairness, Satan's goal is that your marriage suffers spiritual and relational separation by any means necessary.

These conflicted couples prioritize image management over heart restoration.

The apostle Peter best captures our real Adversary's persistent hunt for your marriage in First Peter 5:8: "Your adversary the devil prowls around like a roaring lion, seeking someone to devour." Satan is the one who is keeping your marriage from reaching a higher level with God. In chapter 3 of this book, we will examine in greater detail the psychological warfare Satan levies against your marriage. For now, consider Peter's admonition contained in the first sentence of that same verse: "Be sober-minded; be watchful" of your real adversary (5:8).

There is, however, a greater caution. You cannot, of your own accord, withstand Satan's relentless assault on your marriage. The pressure is too great for your human capacity and mine. Your marriage may withstand it for a season; but eventually you will stumble in your faith, and your marriage will suffer its effects. Left to your own devices, Satan's divisive strategies will prevail.

Of course, the beauty of your faith is that Christ, through His death and resurrection, has already defeated Satan. You need not rely on your own strengths. Satan's idle threats are powerless against Christ's providential plans for your marriage. Satan knows full well that he is a defeated foe against all who carry the Lord's banner. Therefore, he concocts a game plan to keep us behaving in a stupor—as if we are ignorant of Christ's already accomplished work. In other words, Satan's strategy for spiritual and relational separation is to strip our faith of its true power.

A Form of Godliness

The Adversary does not care if you have a washed-out faith. In fact, he encourages this, because it lulls us into a false sense of security. The apostle Paul warns against such hypocrisy when describing those "having the appearance of godliness, but denying its power" (2 Tim. 3:5). Evidences of these powerless marriages are all around us.

Consider how so many Christian couples, with a clear love for Christ, seem totally inept when it comes to marriage. Countless marriages among the faith community languish under a wave of doubts and disappointments. I have seen couples walk out of an amazing and worshipful service, clearly touched by the Lord's presence, only to find them unleashing a barrage of criticism at one another just ten minutes later.

I have sat with couples in ministry leadership who strain to have meaningful conversations with one another when they are out of public view. A faithful marriage requires more than attending church, reciting Scripture or praying the rosary (for my Catholic friends). A thriving marriage requires an active and progressive faith, where spiritual and relational maturity happen in parallel. Spiritual and relational maturity are inseparable.

Too often, however, Christian couples struggle with hypocrisy as they compartmentalize their spiritual walk from other areas of their lives. Thinly veiled smiles plastered across faces in church quickly give way to scowls before the car even gets out of the church parking lot. Sadly, these conflicted couples prioritize image management over heart restoration. The longer the deceit continues, the higher the stakes feel and the deeper the emotional chasm becomes.

As a result, a large segment of the Christian community's integrity and gospel witness is diminished under a shroud of lying, stealing and other sinful atrocities. Not surprisingly, their marriages languish as well. Many divorce when the frustration overwhelms them.

Others stay unhappily married because the consequences of divorce seem too difficult for them or their children to bear. Sin leaves so many of our marriages with deep emotional and relational battle scars that are constant reminders of Satan's disdain for us.

With a quiver of dangerous terms like "irreconcilable differences," "incompatibility" and "hopeless" at his disposal, Satan strives to convince you that the scars of your marriage are too deep for God to heal, proof of its inevitable defeat. He hopes to shame your faith and marriage by pointing out your failures. Satan wants you to believe that the distance between where you are today and where God promises it to be is too great.

True to form, Satan is a liar. God has a different plan—one built on a foundation of grace. A.B. Simpson says it best: "It is not that God will make the good better, but that He will make the bad good, and the utterly and hopelessly bad divinely pure and holy."[3]

Whether your marriage is soaring or sullen right now, God desires to strengthen your faith and lift your marriage as a witness of His glory. Your plight is not your peril but a compass toward the pleasure of God's promise.

Covenant Love

This chapter began with a young Christian couple at the altar, and so it shall end in similar fashion. This is the simultaneously heart-warming and tragic story of Ian and Larissa Murphy, a western Pennsylvania couple. Like Dalia and I, this young couple also met in college.

They, like us, were head over heels in love. After only ten months of what Larissa calls "dating very intentionally," the plans were crystallizing for a short engagement and then marriage soon after finishing college. Ian had dutifully been shopping for the highly anticipated engagement ring. They felt on top of the world, much like Dalia and I felt on our wedding day nearly twenty years earlier. Tragically, everything was about to change.

A thriving marriage finds love equally resilient in the dark places.

For Larissa, it began with a phone call a mere three months before their much-anticipated graduation. On his way to work, Ian was involved in a horrendous car accident that left him with a traumatic brain injury. As Larissa later writes, we "watched our future crash with him in that white station wagon."[4]

The severity of Ian's disability left him incapable of even basic communication. Was all lost? No one would have questioned Larissa's decision to move on to pursue her dreams for career and family. She had every right to want a "normal" life. She and Ian were not even yet engaged. But rather than run, Larissa chose to face uncertainty and her fears to do what many might deem unthinkable. She moved into Ian's parents' home to help care for her best friend. It took four years before Ian could sufficiently communicate for them to feel confident with marriage. Then, as if they had not endured enough, they had to convince the court that Ian was even capable of independently making the decision for marriage.

> Marrying Ian meant that I was signing on to things that I don't think I ever would've chosen for myself—working my whole life, having a husband who can't be left alone, managing his caregivers, remembering to get the oil changed, advocating for medical care, balancing checkbooks, and on. The practical costs felt huge, and those didn't even touch on the emotional and spiritual battles that I would face. But in light of all the practicals, and emotionals, it was so very simple: we love each other. And we love God. And we believe He is a sovereign and loving God who rules all things.[5]

As I consider the beauty and sorrow in Ian and Larissa Murphy's amazing story, I am inspired by the true power of love in the midst of circumstances that seem so unfair. It is not the love of storybooks or fairy tales, nor is it the love of convenience or neediness. Rather, it is love that conquers all because it flows from a divine source. It is love that believes.

As I wrestled to bring to life the immense power of this book's underlying message, the Lord directed me to *This Momentary Marriage*, a book by John Piper. Piper offers a simple yet powerful thesis that our responsibility as a married couple is "mainly about displaying the covenant-keeping love between Christ and His church."[6]

Covenant-keeping love suggests that as we "make of marriage mainly what God designed it to be, no sorrows and no calamities can stand in our way. Every one of them will be, not an obstacle to success, but a way to succeed."

Therein lies the irony. Our Adversary wants you, the Murphys and me to believe that our suffering, difficulties and failures are proof that marriage is hopeless and doomed. Satan wants you to accept the mediocrity of your marriage's comfort zone rather than pushing for supernatural growth. I want to encourage you that nothing stands in the way of your successful marriage except that which you believe—your faith. If you as a couple believe that your marriage is destined for greatness, so it is.

Conversely, if you believe your marriage is maxed out, well, you have indeed set its ceiling. So, what do you believe? My prayer is that your faith will be strengthened to believe that God has more for you.

During the good times, it feels easy and natural to love God and your spouse, but what about when things go wrong? What about when everything seems so unfair? A thriving marriage finds love equally resilient in the dark places.

Despite our vast differences and our history of emotional wounds, Dalia and I are blessed to joyously celebrate more than twenty-seven years of marriage because we share a love and a faith that are not of this world. As explained so well by Larissa Murphy, "We are able to love each other . . . with a more Christlike love."[7] Therein lies the ultimate purpose and tale of two marriages. Marriage with its highs and lows is a God-sanctioned tool to develop success in life and in faith by embracing Christlike love a little bit better.

2

Membership Has Its Privileges

Life is a gift and it offers us the privilege, opportunity, and responsibility to give something back by becoming more.

—Anthony Robbins

From 1987 to 1996, American Express ran a successful campaign around a simple slogan: "Membership has its privileges." I remember receiving my green American Express card while I was still in college, with little in the way of discretionary buying power. Still, I felt proud to carry the card in my wallet because I perceived it as a symbol of achievement. The power of the campaign was the pedigree that it invoked.

American Express wanted their cardholders to see themselves as people of premier status—with select access to special rewards, services and events. In addition, with its buyer's assurance plan, we could have confidence that the power of American Express was solidly behind our purchases. Now, nearly thirty years after this specific campaign ended, I still relish the membership privileges of my American Express card.

Being a Christ follower also has its privileges—ones imminently greater than what American Express promises. Yes, of course, there is most importantly the promise of eternal life with Christ. That is a reward to which I have aspired since I was a young boy. I and millions of other Christians long for that day when the trumpet sounds, and we hear our names read from the Lamb's Book of Life (see Rev. 20:15). Our Christian "membership" assures us that life is not our final home but a waypoint along this journey back to our Creator. We will one day shed these mortal bodies and put on immortal ones, allowing us to bask in the glory and worship of God forever. There is no greater privilege.

All-Access Pass

But Christian membership has privileges on this side of heaven as well. As card-carrying Christians, we can have confidence that God works all things together for good (see Rom. 8:28), that "we are more than conquerors" (8:37), and that no weapon formed against us will prosper (see Isa. 54:17). Collectively, these affirmations offer us something like a spiritual buyer's assurance plan that guarantees us that with faith all things are possible (see Mark 9:23). What have we done to earn such unprecedented privilege? Nothing. So, here is the big picture. By choosing to accept Christ as Savior, we have access to an eternal home with the Father and unlimited access to God's grace now. We have an All-Access Pass.

You may have been to a conference or other event in the past where you either purchased or were given an All-Access Pass. This pass permits you to enjoy everything the event has to offer, carte blanche. Little, if anything, is off limits to you. The unfettered opportunity of an All-Access Pass is an excellent metaphor for your Christian membership.

You have the power to invoke the name of Jesus Christ Himself on behalf of yourself and others. You have direct access to the same Christ who healed the sick, the lame and the blind. Your

Christian membership validates your right to expect Christ to honor His promise to do anything that you ask in His name (see John 14:14).

As chapter 1 connotes, Satan knows about your All-Access Pass. He, however, wants you to downgrade your access status. Imagine having an All-Access Pass to an event but never leaving the lobby to take advantage of your VIP benefits. Yes, you were present, but you settled for an experience far below what you were promised. Satan's plan is to keep you in the proverbial lobby rather than enjoying the front row seat that is rightfully yours. And such is the case for far too many marriages.

We need a paradigm shift in what we believe about our marriages.

One Flesh and the Four-Minute Mile

The benefits of Christian membership's All-Access Pass extend to every facet of life. There is, however, no greater demonstration of its fringe benefits than the relationship that Scripture invokes to describe Christ's relationship with the church. Speaking to husbands and wives in the book of Ephesians, Paul said, "This mystery is profound, and I am saying that it refers to Christ and the church" (Eph. 5:32).

It is indeed profound, and somewhat intimidating, to consider how our marriages mirror Christ's relationship with the church—a relationship Paul dubs "one flesh" (5:31). That responsibility seems so unrealistic, given the trail of failures we've experienced over the decades. I don't feel that I can measure up to the task. When

Dalia and I disagree, I sometimes let my emotions and selfishness get the better of me. Certainly, I am more selfless than I used to be. I care for my wife so much more today than in those younger years. I love her so much deeper than I did at the altar all those years ago. But rarely do I feel that I've satisfied that one-flesh standard modeled after Christ and the church.

We tend to think that God doesn't *literally* mean what Scripture suggests. Since a one-flesh relationship feels too unrealistic, we reinterpret it so that it fits better with our human sensibilities. We contextualize it into an aspirational goal for our marriage that is admirable and honorable—but, in reality, one that we never actually expect to reach. A one-flesh marriage becomes, ostensibly, a fairy tale, a feel-good fable eliciting nods and smiles but little goal-directed commitment.

They stumble and fall, but they never stop believing in the growth of their marriage.

The Christian community has embraced this lie, which is ultimately a deception of the Adversary. Christlike marriage has become our own relational version of what the four-minute mile represented to runners until 1954, an impressively lofty standard that is great to pursue but simply beyond human possibility—until it was proven wrong.

For many years, runners tackling the signature one-mile (1,609 meters) race faced the same question, "How fast can I finish?" Across many continents and among different people groups, no record of someone running one mile in less than four minutes had existed. Yes, the best runners in the world had tried and failed. With such a storied history of failed attempts by the best runners humankind had to offer, conventional thinking became clear—humans could not run a mile in under four minutes. It was simply impossible . . . or so it was thought.

This thinking prevailed until May 6, 1954 when Englishman Roger Bannister did the impossible with an official time of 3 minutes and 59.4 seconds. The four-minute mile barrier was forever broken. With the mystique of impossibility vanquished, two competing runners both clocked a time less than four minutes within a mere two months. Ten years later, a high school junior broke the four-minute barrier. Today, the four-minute mile is normal for elite runners.

How did our understanding of what is possible transition so quickly from impossible to being broken three times within a three-month period? The answer lies simply in the power of belief. In so many ways, belief makes the impossible possible. Once the myth of impossibility is dismissed, a mind shift occurs across the culture. Once the world saw Bannister's feat, minds quickly opened to a new paradigm.

What can we learn about a one-flesh marriage from history's lesson on the four-minute mile? A Christ-centered, one-flesh marriage is not beyond your grasp. It's not an impossible aspiration. Culture needs to see couples actually live out such marriages. Humanity needs to witness husbands and wives who wholeheartedly serve one another out of reverence for God. Time is of the essence.

In a study conducted in 2008, the Barna Group observed a disturbing trend in young adult perceptions about marriage.

> Interviews with young adults suggest that they want their initial marriage to last, but are not particularly optimistic

> about that possibility. There is also evidence that many young people are moving toward embracing the idea of serial marriage, in which a person gets married two or three times, seeking a different partner for each phase of their adult life.[1]

But we don't really need research studies to tell us that God's plans for marriages are being assailed and replaced by mythical presumptions. We need a paradigm shift in what we believe about our marriages. Facilitating that shift is the purpose of this book. We will meet couples who aren't perfect, but who are to marriage what Roger Bannister was to the four-minute mile.

Through their imperfect stories, we will sense a countercultural commitment to believe in the possibility of an extraordinary, one-flesh marriage. Through their stories we will be convinced that our dreams can become reality. We will come to believe in marriage with unbounded growth.

The Growth Mindset

In her book *Mindset: The New Psychology of Success*, Dr. Carol Dweck presents two contrasting mindsets that characterize our human experience and, by association, our marriages. One she calls the *growth mindset*, which is "based on the belief that your basic qualities are things you can cultivate through effort."[2]

When couples operate from a growth mindset, they believe "that their true potential is unknown (and unknowable)" because of the inability to gauge the ultimate impact of their marriage.

Couples with a growth mindset might say to themselves, "the sky is the limit," because one or both parties believe that God has a marvelous plan for their marriage. Out of obedience to God and a desire for fulfillment, they feel compelled to pursue their best. They stumble and fall, but they never stop believing in the growth of their marriage. In contrast, Dr. Dweck argues that couples with a *fixed mindset* believe that their abilities and opportunities as a couple are essentially set in stone.

A couple with a fixed mindset might be heard saying, "We're just playing with the cards we were dealt." You can almost feel the implied resignation. Things simply are what they are. They do not see that attitude is a choice.

In this fixed-mindset marriage, one or both parties allow their limitations and struggles to set a ceiling on their possibilities. Their focus, even in good times, is on their daily grind. For them, dreaming about a future feels frustrating, because they have difficulty even staying on the same page in the present when things are relatively clear.

They believe their marriage belongs foremost to God.

This distinction between the growth and fixed mindset is critical to the success of your marriage. Growth-minded marriages consistently look for opportunities to improve their relationships and their impacts. These couples have the maturity to consistently rebuff Satan's subversive efforts, whereas fixed-minded couples struggle with issues of identity and purpose.

Fixed-minded marriages tend to interpret their lives from a "glass half empty" perspective. They lament about what they don't have and become mired in negativity and self-limiting beliefs.

The Lord challenged me to consider which type of marriage I want for myself and my wife. And, of course, I strive for the growth-mindset marriage. But what I want or intend is not the issue. As Andy Stanley (senior pastor of the Atlanta megachurch North Point) posits, our *direction*, not our intention, determines our destination. Rev. Stanley calls this the "principle of the path."[3] It isn't enough to desire a growth-minded marriage. You have to set your faith in that direction. You have to believe and claim that growth marriage for yourself, regardless of what the Adversary might otherwise suggest. The growth mindset is a fringe benefit to every couple wielding their All-Access Pass.

Meet the Browns

To illustrate the concept of a couple living a growth-minded marriage, I introduce you to Ken and Charmian Brown. One need only spend a few moments with them to sense that they share something that eludes most married couples.

Even after twenty-seven years of marriage, they playfully interact like newlyweds. Whenever I spend time around them, they always seem to enjoy each other's company. The maturity of their relationship exudes confidence—they seem to know that no difficulty is too challenging for them.

Yet, all of these strengths fail to capture their most distinguishing qualities: unquenchable faith, mutual respect and selfless generosity, even in the midst of their own family difficulties. Even when feeling disoriented by blended-family stressors, unbalanced church and family life, and exhausting work schedules, Ken and Charmian regain equilibrium by focusing on God's plan for their marriage to serve others.

In fact, I have seen them giving to others so often that I've lost track of all they have done. Like the coordinated moves of a veteran drill team, their faith and respect for one another yield a generosity that seems effortless in lockstep. Whereas other couples at their stage of life are enjoying retirement, Ken and Charmian's growth-mindedness leads them to continue to volunteer more than ever.

Whether serving wives through Charmian's Anointed Wives Luncheon, speaking to men at Ken's men's ministry, or jointly entertaining couples over a delicious Sunday dinner, Ken and Charmian are gurus of faith-inspired giving. And, it's infectious. With a vision of promoting relationships with God and with each other, their nonprofit organization, Marriage Ministry Together, has touched hundreds of marriages. Without question, Kenny and Charmian have "an unfair advantage" that fuels the generous gifts they so readily share.

The Unfair Advantage

When the Lord first placed the idea of the unfair advantage in my spirit, it felt strange as a claim for a married couple, particularly those of us in the Christian tradition. The term "unfair advantage" is most commonly used to describe a competitive edge (gained through legitimate or illegitimate means) that one entity wields over another.

For example, if two neighborhood teams are playing a friendly game of basketball and Basketball Hall of Fame guard Michael Jordan shows up to play with one of the teams, I would consider that an unfair advantage.

When a corporate insider leaks information unavailable to the public so that he or others can profit from a sale or purchase of that company's stock, the Federal Trade Commission penalizes this insider trading for its unfair advantage. I understood how these examples demonstrated an unfair advantage, but I needed the Lord to clarify what He meant for my marriage and yours.

As a believer, you are already assured that the presence of the Holy Spirit positions your marriage to thrive where other marriages fall short. Jesus' words, in John 14:26, assure you of the Holy Spirit's advocacy on your behalf: "But the Helper, the Holy Spirit, whom the Father will send in my name, he will teach you all things and bring to your remembrance all that I have said to you." The Holy Spirit is a comforter. An indwelling Holy Spirit is your advantage against the Adversary.

This advantage, however, is not one you have earned. In fact, you could never earn enough to purchase your All-Access Pass, because the gap is too wide between your sin-laden nature and God's perfect standard.

As you mix all of these ingredients together, you will discover God's grace and generosity toward your marriage.

Only one person, Jesus Christ Himself, could pay the price of your marriage's All-Access Pass. He did that by sacrificing His life more than two thousand years ago on a hill called Golgotha (Calvary).

Couples with an unfair advantage share three fundamental growth-oriented beliefs. First, they believe their marriage belongs foremost to God. With this mindset, they prioritize their faith over their feelings. Their unfair advantage positions them to see their marriage as something with a higher purpose. This drives their belief that their marriage is not about them.

Second, couples with an unfair advantage believe that their spouse is God's gift to shape them into someone better. With this mindset, they value their differences over domination. These couples demonstrate grace toward their differences, whereas other couples may allow their differences to cause dissension in their relationship.

Third, couples with an unfair advantage believe that their marital journey is a gift not only to themselves, but also to others. With this mindset, they prioritize their giving over their getting. These couples have a heart of generosity both toward each other and those God places in their path. In the throes of a culture bent on self-gratification and a scarcity mindset, an unfair advantage accrues from a heart that is thankful for abundant blessings.

Recipe for Your Unfair Advantage

My wife and I enjoy watching the Food Network on television together, and one of our favorite shows is *Chopped*. This reality-based TV show is a cooking contest in which four chefs compete to win a $10,000 prize. They muster the culinary skills to prepare their best three-course meal in a short time span. After each course, three celebrity chefs judge the contestants' food and eliminate one chef per round until only the winner remains.

But, here's the catch—they must prepare each course using only a mystery basket filled with outlandish ingredients. Consequently, the contestants must be prepared for anything. Fortunately, these experienced chefs are so knowledgeable of how the ingredients complement each other that even when things fail to go as planned, they can quickly adjust their approach to deliver an excellent product.

Inevitably, the winners possess two key traits: expert technical skills and the ability to remain composed under extraordinary pressure, as well as the sometimes biting critique of the celebrity chef judges. Winning *Chopped* is hard because there are no recipes. When the start signal is given, these chefs must use their experience, creativity and intuition to guide them.

I recently gazed at a photo of a tantalizing dish of braised chicken with artichokes and olives accompanied by saffron rice and thought, "Yum! I wish I could make this. I bet those *Chopped* chefs could just look at the picture and reproduce it."

I, on the other hand, would only be able to cook such a dish if there was a recipe accompanying the picture. I need to know what the ingredients are and how to prepare them. Without the recipe, this delicious-looking dish would not find its way onto my dining room table.

Marriage shares many similarities with cooking: there may be mysterious ingredients, extraordinary pressures and critical opinions. If we had to build our marriages based on the *Chopped*-model, chopped is exactly what some of us would be! Few, if any, marriages would survive.

Without clear instructions, life's mystery basket would be more than most of us could handle. Couples need a recipe to see how to produce their own growth-minded marriage. And even a description of the marital benefits associated with an activated faith is not enough. So, how do we activate our faith to fully appreciate all of the benefits Christian membership has to offer our marriages?

Thankfully, the Lord has given His people an Advocate in the person of the Holy Spirit. The Father has also given us a recipe for an unfair advantage that moves our marriage and faith to a higher level. That recipe, found in the book of Second Peter, is the focus of this book.

It is the unfair advantage that promises to elevate the marriages of all who commit to it. The unfair advantage is more than an insightful morsel of biblical truth. Rather, it's a system for spiritual and marital growth (you cannot have one without the other) based on the timeless words of the apostle Peter in Second Peter 1:3–11. This passage illuminates the recipe for a growth-minded marriage made possible by an activated faith. Through this passage we see how an activated faith is supplemented by seven grace habits that build progressively upon one another and position you with an unfair advantage over the Adversary. Let's take a closer look.

> His divine power has granted to us all things that pertain to life and godliness, through the knowledge of him who called us to his own glory and excellence, by which he has granted to us his precious and very great promises, so that through them you may become partakers of the divine nature, having escaped from the corruption that is in the world because of sinful desire. For this very reason, make every effort to supplement your faith with virtue, and virtue with knowledge, and knowledge with self-control, and self-control with steadfastness, and steadfastness with godliness, and godliness with brotherly affection, and brotherly affection with love. For if these qualities are yours and are increasing, they keep you from being ineffective or unfruitful in the knowledge of our Lord Jesus Christ. For whoever lacks these qualities is so nearsighted that he is blind, having forgotten that he was cleansed from his former sins. Therefore, brothers, be all the more diligent to confirm your calling and election, for if you practice these qualities you will never fall. For in this way there will be richly provided for you an entrance into the eternal kingdom of our Lord and Savior Jesus Christ.

When examined closely, we can see the system God gives us through Peter's words. Notice it begins with faith—but that is only the beginning. The important message for those of us in the Christian community is that while faith is the starting point, it is not the only point.

An activated faith is far more than simply proclaiming yourself a Christian. An activated faith is not about how many Sundays you have been in church or the number of Bible verses you can recite. An activated faith is not how eloquent your prayer sounds. Yes, each of these is a positive aspect of your Christian experience, but a fully activated faith is much more.

The Unfair Advantage in Marriage

An activated faith is your All-Access Pass to God's riches for your marriage because it incorporates seven graces that tap into the core of what it means to be Christlike. The system proceeds as such: faith, virtue, knowledge, self-control, steadfastness (perseverance), godliness, brotherly affection and, finally, love. While it is important to note the sequence and building aspect of these seven graces, the key is that they must all be present.

To be clear, the unfair advantage is not a legalistic system to judge how good a Christian you are. In reality, each of these graces takes a lifetime to fully develop. Resist the temptation to think that this recipe requires you to master one grace before proceeding to the next.

Rather, it is a grace-based recipe to encourage you to appropriate the full measure of your Christian membership. As Christian and Missionary Alliance founder Rev. Albert B. Simpson wrote in his book *A Larger Christian Life*, "All that God requires in each of us is an opportunity to show what He can do, and to prove over and over again that 'where sin abounded, grace shall much more abound.'"[4]

An activated faith of husband and wife unlocks a marriage's growth possibilities. Think of each grace as another ingredient to fold into the recipe for a thriving, growth-minded marriage. Together these ingredients foster a couple's ability to accept each other's gifts, helping them see their differences as relational strengths rather than conflicts. There is a caveat, though. You can only gain this perspective when God is the focal point of your relationship.

The result is a heightened sense of security and belonging to God that flows into your marriage. As you develop these graces and keep God as your focal point, you will manage conflict in a healthy way and will successfully transition from one goal to another.

Finally, these graces engender mutual affirmation and encouragement with one another. By incorporating these graces into your lives, you will be amazed at the growth in your spiritual connection with the Lord and your physical, emotional and spiritual intimacy with your spouse. As you mix all of these ingredients together, you will discover God's grace and generosity toward your marriage.

Earlier we saw how those professional chefs survived the *Chopped* kitchen through experience, creativity and intuition. Similarly, this Second Peter recipe gives you an advantage in your marriage's metaphorical kitchen; however, you must constantly stay attuned to the Holy Spirit's direction on how to mix these seven grace ingredients in just the right proportion for your spouse. Some recipes must be adjusted to taste. For example, activated faith for your marriage may require a little more perseverance than mine. My marriage, on the other hand, may require more mutual affection than yours. Such adjustments are necessary because your marriage is not a formula. Your needs differ from your spouses, and your marriage's needs differ from that of other couples.

As you handle the seven graces in your marriage, you will benefit from reliance on the Holy Spirit as your dependable sous-chef. Your ability to increase your expression of these ingredients is a sure sign of a deepening relationship with Christ and, most likely, with your spouse as well.

Your task is simply to walk in that authority, aware that you have an unfair advantage over anything Satan throws your way.

Building a marriage that honors God and transforms lives is best done when all of these graces are present in just the right proportion for your specific marriage.

In her newest book, *The Surprising Secrets of Highly Happy Marriages*, author Shaunti Feldhahn affirms the connection between godliness and a thriving marriage. She notes that 53 percent of very happy couples agree with the statement, "God is at the center of our marriage," compared to 7 percent of struggling couples.[5]

Not surprisingly, happy couples attribute their happiness to a focus on God rather than on the ups and downs of the marital relationship. Godliness is the product of an activated faith.

Feldhahn illustrates grace-inspired faith through the inspiring, real-life stories of couples. These couples are not perfect—and that's exactly the point. They are just like you and me. They are, however, what I consider the Roger Bannisters of marriage. They have broken the barrier in pursuit of a one-flesh marriage. Their stories, highlighted through these pages, open those same possibilities to others. Each couple makes a daily decision to exhibit one or more of the requisite graces needed to activate a faith that places God at the center of their marriage. How these couples claim their unfair advantage is great to see. But that would be of limited appeal if we could not glean key principles from their relationships that can guide any aspiring couple to their own dreams.

The beauty is that behind the curtains of success for all of these couples is a system of overarching principles and progressive habits that are within everyone's reach.

No "magic pill" or "secret sauce" exists but, rather, a guarantee that your relationship will reach unprecedented levels of both intimacy and influence if, as a couple, you devote yourselves to a growth-minded marriage.

As a Christ follower with an account marked "paid in full," you have unmerited favor on your life and the relationships that you hold dear. Your faith is your unfair advantage because it operates on principles of grace rather than your human assumptions.

This book highlights seven graces that bring full vitality to your faith and activate your All-Access Pass. Like the gift card that is useless until it's activated, so is faith that is needed to sustain a growth-mindset marriage. By activating your faith, you access an advantage that you don't deserve and a marriage that you do not own.

God's All-Access Pass gives you an unfair advantage to model a growth marriage for a culture that needs to see what one-flesh really means. But don't by any means expect this to come easy. Satan understands the power that you have to develop an intimate relationship with Christ. His mission is to thwart that process by any means necessary. His goal is simply to steal, kill and destroy the purpose in your marriage.

For this subversive activity he invokes the DRAGONS. You will read more about them in chapter 3. For now just know that God has already given you the power through the Holy Spirit to defeat them. In fact, the Lord defeated them with His death on the cross. Your task is simply to walk in that authority, aware that you have an unfair advantage over anything Satan throws your way.

3

Grace and the DRAGONS

Kill the snake of doubt in your soul, crush the worms of fear in your heart and mountains will move out of your way.

—Kate Seredy

Marriage is an extraordinary gift of God's divine nature, manifested as an unconditional covenant between a husband and wife. God created marriage as a covenant relationship where a man and woman of equal value join together to create something invaluable, something bigger than themselves individually. In God's eyes, your marriage represents the most authentic of human relationships.

Here is the issue—Satan does not accept the calling that God has placed on your marriage. Satan's plans to derail God's intentions for you are never-ending, and his destructive intentions are not just about you. He may attempt to mask his ultimate intent by keeping couples focused on the challenges in their own marriages.

However, Satan's grand plan is of epidemic proportions. Ultimately, he desires to destroy the institution of marriage as a whole; and, therefore, he works through legal and judicial efforts to shift culture away from a biblically based view of husband and wife. He proliferates programs in urban centers and beyond to create entitlement programs with marriage disincentives. Under the auspices of "entertainment," he works through the media outlets to develop programming that erodes the sanctity and exclusivity of marriage.

The Adversary's assault is a broadscale conspiracy against marriage simply because God identified it as symbolic of His relationship with the church. As a result, marriage as a divine institution has fallen out of favor and been replaced by a more superficial relationship, primarily aimed at satisfying our personal needs. Even more sobering is the persistence of these troublesome trends among Christian marriages.

Naked but Not Ashamed

God gives us the optimal portrait of the benefits of a Christlike marriage in the very first book of the Bible, with the first marriage in human history. As Christians, we frequently hear the admonition to leave, cleave and become one flesh, which is based on a pivotal passage in Genesis 2:24–25: "Therefore a man shall leave his father and his mother and hold fast to his wife, and they shall become one flesh. And the man and his wife were both naked and were not ashamed." Paul's one-flesh admonition in Ephesians 5:31, which we examined earlier, is borrowed from this verse.

Thoughtful consideration of this Genesis passage reveals insight into God's description for all one-flesh marriages. The goal is to develop marriages modeled after the "naked but not ashamed" relationship that Adam and Eve had before sin's intrusion.

Your unfair advantage positions you with the growth mindset needed to propel you back to where it started—as a naked and unashamed marriage in a garden of bliss. A naked marriage allows expression of one's true feelings because safety and trust abound.

A naked marriage demonstrates love and respect because there is sensitivity to his and her respective needs. A naked marriage feels no shame because this growth-minded couple prioritizes understanding over judgment and forgiveness over guilt.

Sin, however, disrupted this shameless relationship, resulting in a disruptive power shift that changed the marriage dynamic forever. God issues the consequence of sinful disobedience to the woman, "Your desire shall be for your husband, / and he shall rule over you" (Gen. 3:16).

He hopes that a little doubt will disrupt the entire house of cards.

God also struck the core of a man's identity—his labor—noting, "Cursed is the ground because of you; / in pain you shall eat of it all the days of your life; / thorns and thistles it shall bring forth for you; / and you shall eat the plants of the field. / By the sweat of your face / you shall eat bread" (3:17–19). Now, rather than live off the fruit of God's Eden, man will endlessly toil to provide for himself and his family.

These two Genesis passages, of course, suggest a couple of things. First, prior to sin, the husband did not wield control over the wife. In other words, prior to the entrance of sin into the world, the husband-and-wife relationship was more akin to an egalitarian relationship, a partnership of equals.

Second, prior to sin, necessary provisions were divinely provided. The message is simple. God never intended marriage to be about hierarchy, power and control. That is a by-product of sinfulness.

The problem is that the Adversary disrupts your connection to Christ's gift for your marriage. Just as Scripture offers an unfair advantage system to encourage your marriage, Satan has his own system—a system built to destroy your marriage.

As evidence of this debilitating system, couples pepper each other with hurtful barbs, criticisms and contempt. When these negative forces are at play, a hypercritical narrative replaces the naked and unashamed design for marriage.

This negative discourse pushes the couple farther and farther apart mentally, emotionally and spiritually. Sadly, this is the domain in which Satan's system flourishes. I call that pernicious system "the DRAGONS."

The DRAGONS of Marriage

The DRAGONS are the enemies of your marriage. Their power comes from a single source—sin. In fact, the DRAGONS were nonexistent in the earthly realm until Adam and Eve's disobedience in the garden of Eden.

Satan's agenda is clear when he, disguised as a serpent, encourages Eve to disobey God, "But the serpent said to the woman, 'You will not surely die. For God knows that when you eat of it your eyes will be opened, and you will be like God, knowing good and evil'" (Gen. 3:4–5).

Collectively, these lies represent the forces Satan uses to conspire against what God seeks to do with your marriage. They are the DRAGONS—an acronym representing <u>D</u>oubt, <u>R</u>egret, <u>A</u>pathy, <u>G</u>uilt, <u>O</u>bstinacy, <u>N</u>arcissism and <u>S</u>carcity. The DRAGONS are the attitudes and personality traits that marginalize the promise and potential of your covenant relationship. The DRAGONS' objective is to neutralize your unfair advantage through the dual strategy of promoting your self-interests over God and your spouse, and instilling self-limiting beliefs. In this chapter we take a closer look at each of these DRAGONS and their disruptive intent. The better you understand them, the better prepared you are to rebut their lies and stand firm in God's promises to you and your spouse.

Doubt

Satan's key strategy for disrupting marriage is to instill doubt. Consider how the defense attorney goes to extreme measures to magnify a case's minutest detail to introduce just a modicum of doubt into the minds of the jurors.

In fact, the entire defense case might hinge on creating just an iota of doubt. Satan uses a similar approach. He hopes that a little doubt will disrupt the entire house of cards.

Your marriage can never move forward when you continually focus on what is behind you.

We clearly see this strategy at work in his deceitful words to Eve in the garden of Eden when he contradicts God's warning not to eat of the fruit of the tree of the knowledge of good and evil (see Gen. 3:3). The serpent casts doubt by telling Eve, "you will not surely die" from eating the fruit.

Instead, he convinces her that by disobeying God, she'll find enlightenment. In essence, Satan promises Eve that she'll become like God in her ability to know good and evil. His efforts are so effective because they stroke our self-centeredness.

Although Satan sometimes weaves a morsel of truth into his story as tempting bait, his motivation is always deception. His deceptive tactics always start by casting doubt into your mind; and if you bite into his bait, the rest of the DRAGONS follow.

Like a metastasized cancer, doubt destroys your faith—the core of your spiritual and marital identity. As such, it harms your vision for your marriage because it causes you to lose your long-term perspective.

Doubt makes you shortsighted, focusing only on what you can see right in front of you. As doubt infects your mind, the lens through which you experience the world around you is compromised. Your commitment is shaken.

Doubt leaves you questioning whether you married the right person when communication challenges arise. Doubt prevents you from sharing your true feelings for fear that your spouse will take advantage of your vulnerability.

Doubt clouds your belief that God has a marvelous plan for your marriage. As light is to darkness, so faith is to doubt. Paul writes in Hebrews 11:6, "Without faith it is impossible to please him." Therefore, by association, doubt also makes it impossible to please the Lord.

Claiming your unfair advantage requires that you keep the doubts in check. The reality is that marital doubts will sometimes creep into your consciousness. That is natural. The question is, however, how will you respond?

Do not allow doubt to linger. Do not feed into it. Be confident in what God has spoken and invested into your marriage. Surround yourself with people who validate what God is doing through you.

Take positive steps toward your goals. Repeat affirmations to yourself until doubt loosens its grip. As you do, you will naturally tame the rest of the DRAGONS' cohorts.

Regret

If Satan successfully lodges doubt about your marriage into your consciousness, regret soon follows. Regret is a negative emotional state that involves blaming ourselves for a bad outcome, feeling a sense of loss or sorrow at what might have been, or wishing we could undo a previous choice that we made. Regret happens when life falls short of your hopes and expectations.

Sure, we all experience disappointments; but Satan encourages you to ruminate on that disappointment by keeping you and your spouse focused on your past broken promises, financial faux pas and emotional grievances. Regret is disappointment gone rogue.

Marriage is about being mindful about what it takes to make your marriage better today. Building a thriving marriage requires that you and your spouse live in the present and continually plan for the future. Regret stymies this progress by keeping you focused on you and your spouse's past missteps.

The reality is that your marriage can never move forward when you continually focus on what is behind you. The trajectory of your marriage will always follow the direction of your focus. Positive focus yields positive direction. Conversely, negative focus keeps you mired in the challenges of marriage.

Moving your marriage beyond regret requires redemption. That means forgiving your spouse and yourself—and giving up the right to use it against one another. Redemption is a spiritual choice to replace disappointment with hope in something transcendent.

Apathy

Your marriage is always in motion, moving either toward or away from its purpose. Couples often do not realize this truth. If you aren't deliberately directing your marriage to its next level, then you are drifting. While drifting might be a fun way to spend a lazy summer afternoon on the waves at your favorite beach, it is a major threat to your marriage. Apathy is indecisiveness and possibly even procrastination. If apathy is allowed to persist for an extended period of time, it becomes indifference—and indifference (not hate) is the opposite of love.

Apathy imprisons you in your comfort zone. It lulls you into a false sense of security where you believe that everything in your marriage is fine or, at least, good enough.

God did not join you and your spouse to be "good enough." God expects greatness. Greatness, however, never happens by accident. Satan relishes apathy because he wants you to settle short of your promise and allow your marriage to become stale and predictable. How does that happen?

God has stamped your marital mistakes as "paid in full."

It happens when you forget the things that attracted you and your spouse to each other in the first place. Forgotten romance, insensitive remarks and emotional separation are just some of the drift drivers. I call them drift drivers because if they persist long enough, they dampen your marriage's vitality, sometimes irrevocably.

The primary means to combat the drift is by keeping things fresh in your relationship. Do something out of the ordinary that will mean a lot to your spouse. Don't take him or her for granted. Surprise your spouse with something that communicates the value you place on your marriage.

In doing so, you, not the drift, determine your marriage's direction. Your deliberate action to connect with your spouse is a key to the next level of growth in your marriage.

Guilt

Satan is an accuser of your marriage. John describes it this way in the book of Revelation, "The accuser of our brothers has been thrown down, who accuses them day and night before our God" (12:10). Separated from God the Father by a chasm forged by his disobedience, Satan wants our fate to mimic his, so he goes to work on two fronts.

First, he accuses us before God in hopes that God will forsake us eternally.

Second, Satan works on our minds and circumstances, leading us to believe that we're guilty and without real hope.

In marriage there are often things about which we should feel guilty. Some couples struggle with physical or emotional abuse that has rocked their foundation. Other couples feel like they are living as singles because there is so little shared experience unifying them. Still others have extended lapses of time without the intimacy for which they had hoped.

Although many couples have avoided major catastrophic events, their marriage still feels torturous. Like the historical Chinese practice of torture and capital punishment, their marriage feels as if they are suffering a death of a thousand cuts.

I remember years back when we purchased our current home. The sellers were an older couple whose youngest son was just finishing high school.

After all these years of being married and raising several sons, they were selling their home as part of their divorce proceedings.

They had the resilience to endure the pain for the sake of the children; but feeling released from this obligation, they wanted out.

Like this couple, many of us are guilty of "tiny cuts" toward our spouse that cumulatively render the marriage emotionally, and sometimes legally, dead.

There is, however, a bigger point . . . a question in fact: How do you respond to your own marital transgressions? Satan and the DRAGONS do their best to make you feel condemned, convincing you that you are a hopelessly bad person with an equally hopeless marriage.

Satan wants a sense of condemnation to drive a wedge between you and God, and you and your spouse. He accomplishes this by keeping you focused on your limitations rather than God's unlimited power.

God, however, encourages a different response from you. God, through His Spirit, wants guilt to stir a sense of conviction in you and your spouse. God wants conviction, rather than condemnation, to motivate transformation in your marriage. Condemnation is a negative energy that seeks to demean and shame.

As the apostle Paul says, "There is therefore now no condemnation for those who are in Christ Jesus. For the law of the Spirit of life has set you free in Christ Jesus from the law of sin and death" (Rom. 8:1–2). Conviction, however, is a positive energy that recognizes a gap between actual and desired behavior.

Through the power of grace, Christ's work on the cross has released your marriage from any of Satan's misguided efforts to condemn it. As you embrace God's grace and make your best effort to demonstrate it to your spouse, you will experience Christ's redemption for your marriage and see that God has stamped your marital mistakes as "paid in full."

Obstinacy

Obstinacy, or stubbornness, is one of Satan's most destructive tools because it's rooted in a selfish know-it-all mindset that stunts marital unity. One of the most obvious examples is when you're in a verbal sparring match with your spouse, and you continue arguing even when you know you're in the wrong!

Perhaps you refuse to defer to your spouse's preferences or needs just because you want to have things your way. You may even manipulate a situation to prove your point to your spouse in the company of others. Each of these is an example of obstinacy at work. Simply put, obstinacy is being set in your ways and resistant to change. Obstinacy is pride-induced isolation.

The problem, of course, is that marital growth is built on relationships. Marital growth requires learning from your spouse and listening to positive influencers outside of your marriage. Your marriage can only go to a higher plateau as you and your spouse mature to the next level.

That only happens as you learn to be a better spouse. And learning to be a better spouse requires that growth mindset that was discussed in chapter 2. The growth mindset sees differences between spouses as "iron sharpening iron" experiences that raise the marriage ceiling, not a mindset determined to show your spouse that you know best.

Narcissism

The Mayo Clinic defines narcissism as "a mental disorder in which people have an inflated sense of their own importance."[1] Think about Lucifer's fall from heaven. At its most basic, his transgression was a desire to elevate his own importance to that of God's. When Satan approached Eve in the garden of Eden, he again showed his true colors in suggesting that eating the forbidden fruit would make Eve's knowledge equal to God's. Satan has yet to abandon this age-old deceit called narcissism.

While psychologists have an official diagnosis called "narcissistic personality disorder" to describe this mental condition of grandiosity, Christ followers know that narcissism is akin to spiritual separation from God. Any time you prioritize your own desires over God's, you have in essence committed idolatry.

Pastor Rick Warren started his best-selling book *The Purpose Driven Life* with one of my favorite opening lines of all time: "It's not about you."[2] At the core of most marriage problems is a simple truth. Whether or not they are willing to admit it, most people think their marriage is about them, and the Adversary to your marriage does everything in his power to reinforce this errant thinking.

It is, after all, an easy trap to spring with thoughts like, "Am I happy?" "Is this working for me?" "I deserve better than this." When Satan's distortions make us shortsighted, all we think about is *us*. This myopic perspective hinders our marriage from reaching its designed potential.

But when you genuinely embrace the idea that your marriage belongs to God, it gives you a different vantage point. You can see that you are only a steward of this divine relationship. Only then can you accept that your marriage is a divine sacrament that only fulfills its highest promise when it's surrendered to God.

Scarcity

Satan's final deceit in his deadly DRAGONS' attack on your marriage is scarcity. Though it is last, it is by no means least. Scarcity is Satan's magnifier. He uses this scarcity lens to magnify all his other lies. Scarcity is a fixed mindset that assesses your marriage from a deficit perspective, regardless of whether you are in a season of abundance or constraint.

Let me explain. During periods when things are going really well with ample finances, good communication habits, quality time together and even parenting bliss, a scarcity mindset pushes you to keep it all to yourself, even at the expense of others.

No matter how mature your level of faith, you will transgress in your marriage.

Satan discourages you from sharing the resources and experiences you've acquired in your marriage with others out of fear (even irrational fears) that you will somehow be disadvantaged. Satan tells you to get all you can right now because you have to be prepared for all possible unforeseen circumstances, or to keep your blessings private because it is no one else's business.

Conversely, during real or perceived lean times, Satan uses scarcity to keep you anxious and worried as to how you can make it through. You focus on what's missing in your marriage. Sometimes, it's a lack of financial resources.

At other times, it's a lack of communication. Still other times, it feels like a lack of love. A scarcity mindset keeps you focused on what's missing in your marriage and in your life.

In their book *Scarcity: Why Having Too Little Means So Much*, Princeton University professor Dr. Eldar Shafir and Harvard University economist Dr. Sendhil Mullainathan explore research demonstrating how people's minds are less efficient when they feel they lack something. Their studies demonstrate how scarcity consumes your brainpower, or what Dr. Shafir calls your "mental bandwidth," for less important issues, planning and problem-solving. This scarcity mindset can cause a person to become preoccupied with not having enough money and reinforce self-defeating decisions.[3]

A scarcity mindset can not only sabotage your finances, it can also sabotage your marriage by causing you to think that your spouse and your marriage will never be enough to fulfill you.

Regardless of its manifestation in your marriage, the root of all scarcity is discontent—or not being content with what you have, thinking that it's just not enough.

What is the opposite of scarcity? Although most of us immediately think it's abundance, I really appreciate Dr. Brené Brown's illumination in her book *The Gifts of Imperfection: Let Go of Who You Think You're Supposed to Be and Embrace Who You Are:* "For me, the opposite of scarcity is not abundance. It's enough. I'm enough."[4]

It is no wonder that the apostle Paul says in Philippians 4:11–13:

> I have learned in whatever situation I am to be content. I know how to be brought low, and I know how to abound. In any and every circumstance, I have learned the secret of facing plenty and hunger, abundance and need. I can do all things through him who strengthens me.

Paul aptly notes that regardless of his circumstances, he has learned contentment—which is the secret to overcoming scarcity. As Paul notes, this contentment comes from the knowledge that no situation is too big for him with Christ by his side. That, of course, is the admonition for your married life as well. Satan uses scarcity to attack your perception of your marriage's value. But when you confidently assert your sense of contentment with your relationship, in the presence of abundance or lack, you are saying "We're enough" simply because you're confident there's nothing your marriage can't handle with Christ at your side.

Radical Grace

As you learn to activate your faith for your marriage, maintain a vigilant awareness. Earlier, I asked that you consider Peter's encouragement to "be sober-minded; be watchful" (1 Pet. 5:8). The emphasis here cannot be overstated. The DRAGONS' psychological warfare is real.

We have spent this chapter describing the DRAGONS to convey Satan's agenda to systematically destroy your marriage and your self-image. The hope is that through your exposure to the DRAGONS, you can better see his work as a concerted attack, rooted in deceit. Thwarting his attacks on your marriage is almost always a matter of extending grace to your spouse.

Christianity is, above all else, a grace-based faith. Since sin's introduction into our world, our desires naturally drift away from God rather than toward Him. God, however, wants us in close fellowship with Him. It is only God's grace that allows us to stay in good favor with Him because we can never be fully perfect in our own self. I like those bumper stickers I often see that state, "I'm not perfect, just forgiven." In a way, that says it all. Grace says, "You don't have to be perfect." Grace recognizes that you will disappoint. And Christ paid His life to make grace available to us.

This gift of grace, however, comes with a responsibility. It is the responsibility to extend that favor to others. Marriage may very well be the most important relationship in which grace should be extended.

Given that Christ describes His relationship to the church as the Bridegroom (Christ) to His bride (the church), is it any wonder that He expects your own bridegroom-bride relationship to share the same measure of grace that He extends to you. Christ models grace for us to emulate.

Just as in our Christian service, grace in marriage looks like forgiveness and second chances. Grace looks to unleash possibilities rather than stand in judgment. Grace hopes.

They stand no chance against a couple who is determined to live an active, grace-inspired faith.

Graceful couples enjoy their marriage. Of course, it works best when each spouse demonstrates grace to the other; but even when it's one-sided, grace can still transform a marriage.

No matter how mature your level of faith, you will transgress in your marriage. It may not be in the form of an affair or physical abuse; but as I described in chapter 1, it can manifest itself in less obvious ways like not showing empathy to a hurting spouse or being overly critical or self-centered. When it comes to marital transgressions, the list is endless.

Just as in our relationship with Christ, we all fall short at times in our marriage. This doesn't mean you're a bad person or that you don't care about your spouse. It doesn't even mean that you're selfish.

It just means you're human; and the gift of grace is what allows two flawed people to authentically love each other with unquenchable passion. The only question is how radical can your grace become? The more radical your grace, the more rich your marriage. On one level this seems to be a simple notion, but as any couple who's been married for even a few years can tell you, it can be difficult to maintain that grace posture because of the selflessness that it demands. Establishing your faith as the centerpiece of your marriage requires a radical grace centered on what Christ desires your marriage to become.

The Grace Card

In 2011, David G. Evans directed a faith-based movie titled *The Grace Card.*[5] Fueled by a sense of personal responsibility for the death of his young son, the main character harbors anger and resentment that is tearing apart his family and his workplace. Ultimately, he must face his DRAGONS in order to save the life of his remaining son, his marriage and his own soul. In the end, he must decide if he will extend grace (symbolized by a grace card) to the very person that he most hates.

While this is a good scene in a fictitious movie script, real-life marriage is best lived through the liberal use of your own grace card. The grace card is emblematic of your unfair advantage because by definition it represents unearned favor.

The grace card is recognition that the same unmerited favor that God extends to you must be passed along to undeserving others, especially your spouse. The grace card is the membership card that grants you backstage access to Christ and the privileges and full authority available to His followers. Now, here is what Satan fears most—the grace card is your sword to slay the DRAGONS with the love of God. Satan is a formidable adversary to your marriage.

The reality is that the DRAGONS never really go away. God allows Satan and his minions to wield influence on the earth, but they stand no chance against a couple who is determined to live an active, grace-inspired faith. You just have to believe in the One whom you serve, and brandish your grace card with reckless abandon.

To assist you in this regard, each of the seven grace chapters will end with an affirmation of grace that you can exchange with your spouse. Think of them as your own grace cards to keep grace alive in your marriage.

Part 2: The Unfair Advantage

4

Pursue an Active Faith

Faith is a living, daring confidence in God's grace, so sure and certain that a man could stake his life on it a thousand times.

—Martin Luther

I knew something was different about Drs. Wesley and Rose Marie Greene within moments of meeting them for the first time. The very first thing I remember thinking about them was the affection they showed toward each other. It was like watching two teenagers with a crush on one another. When they spoke of their marriage, the authenticity was palpable. It didn't take me long to realize something else about this extraordinary couple. Their marriage was rooted in a deep faith foundation, one that had sustained them through some of life's nastiest challenges, including the death of their son, Rose's difficult battle with cancer, and major business challenges.

Since we first met the Greenes, they have become two of our dearest friends. In fact, we consider them spiritual mentors because they've established their marriage on a foundation of faith. They've shared stories with Dalia and me that are nothing short of miraculous. Buoyed by a litany of biblical affirmations, they trust God's Word regardless of how situations may appear—such as when they believed for God's supernatural intervention in purchasing their lakefront dream house. More importantly, they trust God's Word as a unified front against the DRAGONS. After nearly thirty-five years of marriage, they remain a remarkable couple.

Dalia and I are continually challenged by the Greenes' level of trust in God's provision for their marriage and their family. When we face difficulties in our family and need godly counsel or prayerful intercession, we call Wesley and Rose Marie. And we are not alone.

They are pastors of Amazing Grace World Outreach Church in Forest Park, Georgia, and their congregation looks to them for spiritual guidance as well. They model a level of trust in their marriage that only comes through weathering life's storms.

Without question, overcoming their adversities has forged a solid foundation, with influence far beyond the walls of their church. The Greenes' success can only be understood through a faith lens because that's what sustains and motivates their lives as pastors, as community advocates and as entrepreneurial savants. What is the key to their success?

Faith and Marriage

As I mentioned in chapter 2, the recipe for marriage's "unfair advantage" and activated faith is found in Second Peter 1:3–11. Here God states the seven graces that supplement the activated faith: virtue, knowledge, self-control, steadfastness (perseverance), godliness, brotherly affection and love. Peter introduces the seven graces with the exhortation, "May grace and peace be multiplied to you in the knowledge of God and of Jesus our Lord" (1:2).

As married couples, we must decide how committed we are to an active faith in which the graces are generously shared. The notion of "active faith" is so central to kingdom living (i.e., following Christ) that I would like to explore it a little more as it pertains to marriage.

We have established faith as the centerpiece of Christian marriage. The problem is, however, that many couples' faith is passive. For these couples, faith is a box they check because they believe in God, they attend church regularly and they can recite some Bible verses. Too often, though, these Christian couples see this passive faith as the full measure of what makes a marriage work. They might say, "Faith is all we need," which sounds deeply spiritual but is naive. I cringe when I hear this. My concern is not about the merit of faith, but about its depth.

The single most important thing to grow your marriage is prayer.

Yes, faith is the essential starting point, but growth as a couple requires an *active* faith. This type of faith is buttressed with the seven graces. This more robust faith activates kindness, peacefulness and that unfair advantage in a marriage. To reiterate, faith is just the starting point.

An older couple I know—let's call them Sam and Arnest—is a great example of what I call this faith fallacy regarding marriage. In their years as young Christian adults, Sam and Arnest were taught in church to only marry another Christian.

The attitude of the day was that as long as they were "equally yoked," things would work out. As long as a couple shared the same faith, conventional church wisdom told them that they had the tools to make things work.

Fortunately, Sam and Arnest have been married now for more than fifty years. I certainly admire the commitment they made to staying married; unfortunately, most of their marriage has been a struggle.

They have accomplished much to be proud of in the past five decades. They successfully parented many children, ministered in their local church for decades, and made a significant impact in their community.

But, in spite of these accomplishments, they never attained a thriving marriage. Although their faith in God and in Christ's message has clearly been their source of strength throughout the years, it hasn't translated into the deep faith foundation that God desires for their marriage.

The shared elements of their faith have kept them together, but they've lacked the conviction to move their marriage into the higher position of influence that I believe God has for them. Despite enduring fifty years, this couple isn't where they wish, because their faith hasn't matured their marriage to its potential.

Sadly, their story is not unique. I've seen a similar pattern repeat itself far too often. But there is hope for couples who are open to hearing a different message. The church and Christian marriage educators and counselors need to show them how to pursue a grace-inspired active faith that matures their marriage.

They must know that unless they strive to heed the full gamut of Scripture and mature toward the character of Christ, their marriage risks falling short of its full potential. Only when a marriage reaches its full potential can a couple truly escape the DRAGONS and remain poised to claim God's promises (see 2 Pet. 1:4) using their unfair advantage.

Four Decisions Faithful Couples Make

When I have a major concern or need wise counsel, I go directly to the Greenes for spiritual guidance. I depend on their gifts of encouragement and prayerful intercession to touch the heart of God on my behalf.

I believe the key to their success as a couple is their reliance on four faith factors that help elevate their marriage to such a high level of faith: prayer, purpose, service and investment. I hope these four actions will generate your own momentum toward an unfair advantage in your marriage by solidifying your faith foundation.

Pray Together Daily

Without question, the Greenes have shown me that the single most important thing to grow your marriage is prayer. I marveled at the nonstop prayer vigil Wesley embarked upon when Rose Marie was in the hospital with a cancer so aggressive it had taken the lives of others in her cancer support group.

I will never forget Wesley telling me how he stood like a sentinel at his wife's bedside through the darkest of hours, praying for God's hand to pull Rose through this health crisis.

He simply refused to allow the disease to take his beloved wife from him and their family without expending every spiritual resource available to him. His prayer of intercession found favor with God and today Rose is cancer free! So, imagine how it blessed Dalia and me when the Greenes requested a picture of our own family so that they could use it symbolically to pray together on our behalf.

We were honored and elated, especially in light of the challenges our family was experiencing at the time. Their prayers, and those of others, have sustained us through difficult days—and we are not unique in any way. Dalia and I have had the opportunity to encourage many couples regarding growing their marriage. We always prioritize praying together daily. This is critical for many reasons, but I would like to focus on three of them.

- First, daily prayer provides spiritual direction for the Christian couple. When offered with a sense of humility, prayer invites God's will, rather than our own self-centeredness, to be the centerpiece of our attitudes and actions. With a sense of divine direction, couples are more assured that the decisions they make are ultimately best for fulfilling their destiny as a team of two. Daily prayer also forms a hedge of defense against the DRAGONS' spiritual assaults by encouraging couples with positivity and hope.
- Second, daily prayer provides a relational guidepost that communicates the priority spouses have for each other. With the harried lifestyles we lead, couples often struggle to reserve time to really invest in each other; allocating time to pray daily reminds them that what matters most is a couple attuned to God's plan for their marriage.

  To be clear, the prayer does not have to be an elaborate affair that goes on for thirty minutes. The actual length of the prayer is not particularly relevant. The real benefit is how intentionally spending even a few minutes together consistently strengthens your trust bond as it allows each person's respective needs to be best understood.
- Third, daily prayer provides an intercessory channel for the couple to unite on behalf of others, whether this is for family members, friends, coworkers, or others in need of divine intervention. In our own prayer time, Dalia and I spend

more time praying for the needs of others than for ourselves. Sometimes, needs are specific; other times, we are praying for general covering. We believe that the prayers of righteous people have significant consequence (see James 5:16).

Furthermore, we take God at His Word when He says that He will act where two people agree and ask anything in His name (see Matt. 18:19). Many people are hurting and in need of a divine touch. You and your spouse's daily prayer is a conduit for God to pour Himself into their lives. You have probably heard the cliché: "Couples who pray together, stay together." That idiom only captures a portion of the power of prayer. It sounds a bit too passive for my taste. I believe that a faith-centered narrative would be more like this: "Couples who pray together, grow together."

Pursue a Shared Purpose

Couples thrive best when they have a shared goal that pushes them together toward a purpose in which they are mutually invested.

The operative phrase here is "mutually invested," meaning a desire that has an emotional appeal for each of them. So often, the more dominant personality of the marriage ends up intentionally or inadvertently pushing through an agenda that lacks appeal to the spouse.

I have made this mistake in my marriage multiple times because I confused my wife's concession as agreement or maybe even interest in my idea. I, like so many others, am still a work in progress, but I'm grateful that I've made meaningful progress in listening and incorporating my wife's perspective into my own. Developing a shared identity and purpose as a couple demands such mutual accommodation from both spouses. This is the essence of teamwork.

I have not personally seen any couple work as a team better than the Greenes. They work together as entrepreneurs of a business, and they also team up to minister to a vibrant congregation at their Atlanta church. Yet, somehow the Greenes still find time and resolve to pursue their shared interest in encouraging other marriages, especially the marriages of pastors and ministers. They believe that too many ministry marriages are so overly strained by the work of ministry that they inadvertently sacrifice their marriages and families at the altar of church building.

We tap into His unfathomable power that unlocks the doors to abundance.

Their concern for ministry marriages is valid. According to Dr. Richard Krejcir, a survey conducted by the Francis A. Schaeffer Institute of Church Leadership Development revealed that 77 percent of the pastors surveyed (more than one thousand pastors) felt that they did not have a good marriage.

Of that sample, more than one-third admitted they were either divorced or in the process of getting divorced.[1] In response to this disturbing trend, the Greenes have, by faith, taken steps to establish a setting in which ministry couples can retreat for both relationship counseling and relaxation.

For the Greenes, pursuing a shared purpose as a couple builds faith because it fosters a spirit of cooperation rather than one of competition, which so often tears the fabric of marriage. It empowers partnership rather than parallel interests, and it helps them spend meaningful time together—which is important given the abundance of time-starved marriages around them.

Serve the Other

When God created Eve from Adam, His intention was to establish a model for mutual service. Paul masterfully describes a faith-filled marriage in Ephesians 5:21–33. God designed marriage for mutual service. Ephesians 5:25 says that husbands are to demonstrate to their wives the same type of love that Christ shows for the church.

This is a phenomenal, if not formidable, challenge for any husband seeking to obey God's intent. Conversely, Ephesians 5:22 instructs wives to submit themselves to their husbands as unto the Lord. This too can be especially difficult for women who've been disappointed, or even injured, by men in whom they've put their trust.

Ultimately, God models mutual submission in Ephesians 5:21 when He instructs husbands and wives to submit themselves to one another.

There is no greater demonstration of such service than that offered by Jesus Christ. Whether He was washing His disciples' feet, healing the sick or dying for our salvation, the whole of Jesus' existence was to serve. Service is God's channel for connecting human relationships. Whether pertaining to marriages or human relationships, God intends for us to serve one another.

Service can take many forms; encouragement, affirmation and resources are a few examples. At its core, however, service is authentic generosity. It is giving of yourself to help someone else, and often it requires sacrifice. Marriage is designed to be a partnership in which the mutual strengths of each party are leveraged to serve others in a way that neither person could accomplish individually.

Above all else, the Greenes are servants. Even with all of their gifts, I believe it is their servant-hearted nature that is their greatest attribute. They serve as pastors to a congregation that adores them. They have earned the respect of business and nonprofit organization leaders through their integrity and service on a number of boards and committees.

They serve their family (children, grandchildren and parents) with uncompromising devotion. I watched in amazement as they served Wesley's aging father for more than a year until his death. One of their greatest marital challenges was caring for him, initially, long distance—until they moved from Missouri to Georgia to live with him.

During this time, they experienced lengthy separations and a complete dismantling of their regular routine. For the Greenes, a faith-filled marriage looks like service to others.

Invest in Your Marriage

Couples in a faith-filled marriage grow toward one another and God's desire for them as a couple. But this doesn't happen by osmosis or good intentions. A marriage will always move in the direction it faces. Marriages that thrive continually calibrate themselves to align with what they believe God is doing through them as a couple.

This calibration happens through a steady stream of conscious investments in their growth. These investments may take the form of educational resources (marriage seminars, books), relationship accountability (couple's fellowships, a mentoring couple), or just quality time together (date nights, devotionals).

You might think that with such a thriving marriage, the Greenes rest on their laurels. In fact, the opposite is true. They continue to attend marriage-enrichment events, purchase resources and spend time working on their marriage. Their investment continues to pay rich dividends in the quality and impact of their marriage.

The path to a thriving marriage demands that we show kindness to one another so that our marriage is a peaceful one. But as Scripture continues, we only obtain this level of kindness and peace through getting to know God better.

Cultivating a faith culture in your marriage requires a commitment to getting to know Christ better by studying His Word and by doing your best to emulate the kindness and peace of which Peter speaks.

For the Christian couple, the walk with Christ and with one another are tightly connected.

The result is a marriage that truly represents the good life. That good life comes with all the other rich and wonderful blessings that God has promised us. The benefits of this faith walk are twofold: (1) protection from the destruction that surrounds our marriages and (2) the development of our character as a couple. The promise of an active faith is that as we submit ourselves and our marriage to God, we tap into His unfathomable power that unlocks the doors to abundance.

Necessary, but Not Sufficient

Your marriage can experience this power and abundance too, when you see faith as just a starting point for what God desires to accomplish through your marriage. As I have learned from the Greenes, a faithful marriage is more than just reciting encouraging Bible verses, attending church together or even proclaiming salvation—though each of these is good in and of itself. A faithful marriage commits to facing a direction in which the four factors discussed in the preceding pages come alive.

Yet, based on the Second Peter passage, I am convinced that a common faith is still not enough. During my years as a doctoral student, I was exposed to the phrase "necessary, but not sufficient."

This phrase was used to describe a statistical or methodological condition that was required but could not alone explain the phenomenon being observed.

This phrase also works well for the role of faith in marriage. Faith is, without question, an integral component for developing a thriving marriage—but you need more.

Why isn't faith enough? Because our faith in Christ is a work in progress. As people of faith, we are expected to continually mature spiritually toward God's call for us. We are not expected to have arrived when we first proclaim our faith in Christ. We all know that faith is a journey.

The apostle Paul spoke of this maturation in Hebrews 5:12 when he suggested that the Hebrew Christians needed milk rather than solid food because they had not yet developed their understanding of Scripture.

He repeated this idea in speaking to the church at Corinth. He tells the Corinthians that they need milk rather than solid food because they are not yet ready for it (see 1 Cor. 3:2). The message is clear. Faith is a process of maturation.

This same dynamic is relevant to faith in the context of your marriage. Faith is the backbone of your marriage for sure, but the graces must accompany it to mature your faith and, by association, your marriage.

So, is your marriage still "milky" or is it ready for solid food? As a Christian couple, your marriage will never go farther than your faith can carry it. Your faith creates a desire for a closer walk with Christ which, in turn, challenges you to a closer walk with your spouse. For the Christian couple, the walk with Christ and with one another are tightly connected. You cannot have one without the other.

Over the next seven chapters, you will see exactly what it means to activate your faith with each of the graces mentioned at the end of chapter 2.

5

Invest in Virtue

Courage is not simply one of the virtues, but the form of every virtue at the testing point.

—C.S. Lewis
The Screwtape Letters

The next step in your grace-inspired journey toward your unfair advantage begins when you clearly sense which direction your faith is leading you. After extolling the importance of faith, Peter builds upon it in his Second Peter 1:5 instruction when he states simply, "make every effort to supplement your faith with virtue." What is Peter telling us about godly living through this instruction?

A Virtuous Marriage

The profession of faith necessitates pursuit of Christlike character. It is no wonder that Scripture tells us that without faith it is impossible to please God (see Heb. 11:6). Faith is the force that motivates you to be a person of character or virtue or, simply put, a person of goodness or moral excellence. Putting these ideas together, we can see that virtue is a faith enhancer because it extends the tenets of your Christianity into the essence of your character. As my father, the Reverend Harold Arnold Sr., preaches to anyone who will listen, virtue results from the person of Christ dwelling within you. In other words, your character gives human form to your faith. Indeed, Scripture tells us that Christ's presence within us is the hope of glory (see Col. 1:27). And certainly Christ's presence within you is the hope for your marriage.

All goodness comes from the Lord who rules over heaven and earth. That's why Peter's instruction to supplement your faith with good character is important for your marriage. Marriage at its most basic is more about the person you are becoming and less about who you were when you married.

Their one-flesh prayer and worship time . . . keeps them connected through life's ups and downs.

In fact, the fire of marriage actually forges virtue. In a virtuous marriage, a couple's desire to live for Christ motivates them to give their best individually to build a marriage that is defined by devotion to God, one another, family and beyond. A virtuous marriage isn't perfect; however, it is marked by a pursuit to be the best couple that you can be.

I visited a glass factory while vacationing in South Africa. As I walked through the retail portion of the factory, I admired the glassware's artistry. Glass was shaped into such African animals as elephants, giraffes and warthogs.

Colorful jewelry was on display, as well as glasses, vases and many other artifacts. What I appreciated most about the visit, however, was being allowed to watch the artistic process from the observation deck. Watching the artists make beautiful glasswork by repeatedly firing and shaping it was amazing. What the artists were creating was not obvious at the beginning of the process. But, as they continued the spinning, shaping and firing process, the artifact became recognizable as a fish or a vase or something else. Marriage is something like glassmaking. God is the master craftsman.

Only He initially knows what He intends you and your spouse to become, both as individuals and as a couple. Discerning what God is crafting early in the marriage process can be difficult; but if we remain flexible, God can shape us and our marriage. Just as the glassmaker uses fire to keep the glass pliable, God uses life's fiery situations to make us receptive to what He desires for us. In other words, neither your character nor your marriage can take on the shape of God without experiencing difficulties.

Undoubtedly, marriage is part of the firing and shaping process that God uses to craft you into the masterpiece He intended from the beginning of time. No other human relationship can shape your character as powerfully as marriage. Submitting yourself to this shaping process is not easy.

It pushes you out of your comfort zone. It challenges your assumptions. It demands more of you. And, as C.S. Lewis writes, this demand—or testing—always requires you to be courageous.[1]

Under His Wings

Chris and Juanita Gissentaner needed a lot of courage to develop virtue in their marriage. By all intents and purposes, the native New Yorkers had lived a very successful life together. After thirty-eight years of marriage, they had successfully raised six children who all actively shared their Christian faith, and they were the proud grandparents of seven grandchildren.

In addition, they were respected leaders in a local ministry and had climbed the ladders of success in their careers. Chris held a secure management position with a lumber company, and Juanita worked in special education for a secondary school. Although they weren't perfect by any means, Chris and Juanita had so much to be proud of—and they were. With those once-distant retirement years and the accompanying relaxed lifestyle now clearly within sight, the two were ready to rest on their laurels.

Then something stirred within Chris' spirit that wouldn't let go. An audacious dream lit an almost frightening fire inside him. Yes, he had many more questions than answers. Even more daunting, once he summoned enough courage to actually believe the possibility of his dream, he had to share it with Juanita. That was going to be a tough sell—or so he expected.

His cautious wife refused to budge on some of Chris' previous business ideas, so Chris knew this latest idea would only happen if it was from God. He took almost a year to perceive the "right time" and then mustered the courage to introduce the idea to Juanita. Encouraged through prayer, he finally proposed his idea to her with bated breath. It was about marriage—but not just their marriage. And it required retiring from their stable jobs earlier than planned and selling their home in Long Island, New York, an area that had been their haven for nearly twenty years.

Chris explained to Juanita that their house would be replaced by another one—and not just any house. No, they would design this house themselves with a specific ministry in mind: a respite and ministry center for married couples of all kinds. Located about three hours away from New York City's hustle and bustle, in the Catskill Mountains, this house would accommodate up to six couples at a time.

Here crisis couples would find light in their dark places, and strong couples would rejuvenate from life's stresses. And—perhaps the most courageous part of the move—running the house would be their full-time job, their sole source of nonpension income. Chris' vision would be called Under His Wings Ministries.

This time Juanita's reaction was a pleasant surprise, confirming the Holy Spirit's movement. In fact, she bubbled with palpable excitement about the adventure that Under His Wings Ministries offered them as a couple.

In a word, a virtuous marriage is characterized by wholeness.

Furthermore, Juanita saw it as an opportunity to help other couples achieve a level of unity that had eluded them for much of their own marriage, as they battled through emotionally volatile blended-family issues.

Both Juanita and Chris believed Under His Wings Ministries would become a spiritually vibrant prayer and worship station for couples—starting with themselves!

Dalia and I have known Chris and Juanita for several years now. As I think back to my initial phone call with them, I remember the sound of authenticity and empathy in their voices. I knew they were the real deal. Since that conversation, I've visited their respite, called the Restoration Nest, several times with different groups of couples. I've also had the opportunity to attend their marriage seminars.

Regardless of the setting in which you encounter Chris and Juanita, you are always struck by the self-effacing warmth of their personalities, the strength of their faith, the integrity of their character, and Chris' corny humor (but we won't count that one).

We have personally benefited from the hospitality, enrichment and encouragement proffered through Chris and Juanita's work. If it were a fairy tale, maybe I could tell you that their leap of faith has been smooth sailing; but that hasn't been their experience. For sure, Chris and Juanita's pursuit has been successful by the most important measures.

Their own marriage has grown, which they attribute to their one-flesh prayer and worship time that keeps them connected through life's ups and downs. The number of marriages enriched by their ministry has also steadily increased. They recently published their first book together entitled *Spouse-ology: Developing and Nurturing an Intimate Marriage.*[2] Most importantly, they've become people of tremendous integrity and character.

Chris and Juanita will be the first to tell you that they have struggles in their marriage just like the rest of us. Yet, in spite of their shortcomings, they personify what Peter describes in Second Peter 1:5 as the virtue that makes their faith tangible. When a couple enters the doors of the Restoration Nest, they might not describe the experience as virtuous, but for most couples virtuous is exactly how they feel.

Tangible Faith

In the last chapter, we described faith as the cornerstone for Christian marriage. In Second Peter 1:5, we see that virtue, or character, helps bring your faith to life. Think of faith as a spiritual stream that flows through and sustains your marriage. Virtue, then, is the visible manifestation of that sustenance. Virtue is the way others experience the flow of the Holy Spirit between you and your spouse. Virtue reflects the true matters of your heart as a couple—the real you beyond any social facade. Your virtue is your true identity as a couple. You may act out of character for a short period of time, but the real heart of your marriage ultimately comes through, whether you like it or not.

Virtue as Wholeness

Realizing your unfair advantage requires faith that is supplemented by virtue, or what I call a virtuous marriage. So how can you claim your own virtuous marriage? The answer is: with integrity. In fact, for a thriving marriage, virtue and integrity are synonymous.

The term "integrity" conjures up many thoughts. Terms like authenticity and honesty most readily come to mind. While these are appropriate terms to associate with integrity, I would like to offer an additional one—wholeness. In a word, a virtuous marriage is characterized by wholeness.

Before I explain this idea more fully, I'd like us to examine a well-known biblical incident involving Jesus, which powerfully communicates virtue as wholeness. In Mark 5:25–34, we are introduced to a woman with what is described in the King James translation as an "issue of blood." We don't know the exact nature of her illness, but contemporary medicine might diagnose her with menorrhagia, which is an abnormal and excessive bleeding at menstruation.

From this condition, she was likely to have severe anemia, rendering her weak, frail and highly prone to acquiring other immunologic conditions. Although the medical details were scant, we are told that her condition had worsened despite having spent everything she had on physicians.

The woman wanted to be healed; and she believed that if she could simply touch Jesus' clothes, she would be "made whole." So, as Jesus passed through a large crowd of people, she indeed managed to touch the hem of his garment and was immediately healed. But the story doesn't stop there. Jesus actually stopped and asked who in this large crowd had touched him, which baffled His disciples given the vast number of people surrounding them. I imagine that they also must have wondered, "What difference does it make?"

Alignment means that you insist on staying harmonious as a couple.

But Jesus told them that virtue, or power, had transferred from Him to her with that touch. She was fearful of confessing what she had done, which was culturally inappropriate particularly given her disease; but Jesus said to her, "Daughter, your faith has made you well; go in peace, and be healed of your disease" (Mark 5:34).

The King James translation actually says "thy faith hath made thee whole." The sequence of events here is powerful. The woman's faith pushed her to reach out for Jesus, which in turn unleashed the virtue that made her whole. This is the same sequence that Second Peter invokes when adding virtue to faith.

Wholeness is comprehensive. Wholeness challenges every facet of your marriage to be characterized by authenticity and truthfulness. An attitude of wholeness challenges each spouse to be wholly who God makes him or her to be.

Wholeness means that every aspect of your marriage is subject to what God calls it. Wholeness means a congruency between your spiritual ideals and your natural walk. Where there is wholeness, there is no room for hypocrisy. There is no place for compartmentalizing one's attitudes or actions. Wholeness requires that your spirituality be fully integrated into everything that you do in life, including your marriage.

In John 5:5–6, Jesus asked a man who had been lame for thirty-eight years, "Do you want to be healed?" Why would Jesus ask such a question? Most of us would think it's obvious that after being lame for such a long time, he would desire healing. However, there seemed to be something instructive in Jesus' question, which pushed the lame man to consider honestly his deepest fears and desires.

I wonder if it might also be helpful to consider this question for our marriages. Do you truly want your marriage to be made whole, or are you just giving it lip service? If you desire a virtuous marriage, you must first desire yourself to be made whole.

Virtue requires integrity or wholeness. Your actions and attitudes must consistently reflect your faith mantra. When Peter encourages us to supplement our faith with virtue, he is instructing us that our faith must permeate the entirety of who we are because we know *whose* we are.

The Virtue Investment

I speak about virtuous marriages, but how do we really assess our virtue? Isn't virtue too abstract to measure? One of the clearest methods of assessing the virtue, or wholeness, in your marriage is to look at where you allocate your resources, time and money. That's the simplest barometer of what is important to you and the core of who you are as a couple. Scripture says it this way, "For where your treasure is, there your heart will be also" (Matt. 6:21). Does your investment of time and money consistently reflect what God has ordained for your marriage?

For example, couples with a heart for material wealth spend their time acquiring houses, cars, clothes, jewelry and other things that satisfy this desire. Couples with a heart for children devote themselves to bringing joy to those children. Some couples, like my friends Norman and Cynthia Brown, have a gift for hospitality. This is their virtue.

When you enter their home, you feel genuinely loved and cared for. My sister Mina Handy and her husband Valdimir demonstrate virtue in the generous way they share their home with others in need of housing arrangements. I've lost count of the number of family members, friends and relative strangers that have called their house home.

Of course, my wife and I have a heart to help couples improve their marriages. We strive to show virtue in the way we encourage couples. As you may surmise, we spend much of our discretionary time teaching relationship skills.

These are just a few examples of virtue at work in marriage. The challenge for each of us is to make sure these priorities are wholly integrated into who we are as Christians and as a team of two. This is the best demonstration of an active faith supplemented by virtue.

Stay Aligned as a Couple

Chris and Juanita Gissentaner helped me to understand that the first rule of a thriving marriage is learning to stay on the same page. Alignment doesn't necessarily mean agreeing with every decision. Frankly speaking, there will be instances when you vehemently disagree with your spouse's preference or approach.

That's okay. Alignment is more about the posture that spouses take in relation to each other.

Alignment means that you insist on staying harmonious as a couple even when you see things differently than your spouse. Alignment means that you don't rest as a couple until your energies are flowing in the same direction. It *does* suggest that both sides agree with a particular direction or goal as a team or partnership.

As an example of this, Chris and Juanita highlight how their own freedom as a couple did not come until they agreed to talk more deliberately to one another, pray together, and then take the time to make decisions together—even the seemingly simple decisions.

I choose to invest my full energy to demonstrate godly virtue and remain aligned as a couple.

It isn't always easy for couples to align around a common pursuit. This difficulty is due to differences in personalities and interests, making it challenging to pinpoint a shared identity that resonates with both husband and wife. But when couples find that point of agreement that fits God's purpose for them, they possess tremendous power as a team of two. Discerning that point of agreement is a major step toward pursuing your identity as a couple.

If the faith stream of your marriage roars like raging rapids, then everyone around you will be strengthened by the authentic way you and your spouse love and interact with one another. Authenticity becomes the calling card of your marriage. Such authenticity rebuffs shame and unworthiness.

Conversely, if the faith stream of your marriage is more akin to a trickle, you will struggle to consistently exemplify the integrity that makes your faith tangible. Your marriage becomes unpredictable, erratic and overwhelmed.

Your virtue influences the way people experience you. People do not directly experience your faith—they experience your character. A thriving marriage is a virtuous enterprise based on the strength of a couple's character. Couples can never achieve extraordinary results without extraordinary character. Character, demonstrated through authenticity, transparency and mutuality, is the evidence of virtue, providing you with the tools to stay God-centered through the ebb and flow of life and marriage.

Virtue's Grace Card

I choose to invest my full energy to demonstrate godly virtue and remain aligned as a couple, even when our differences and circumstances challenge the character of our marriage.

6

Empower Knowledge

The larger the island of knowledge, the longer the shoreline of wonder.

—Ralph W. Sockman
Now to Live!

With faith as the backbone of your relationship and virtue as your calling card, your marriage is in a prime position to influence God's kingdom. Faith and virtue demonstrate an openness to follow God's direction as a couple. If not for Peter's continued instruction, we may be inclined to believe that these two elements are enough for a thriving marriage. But, Second Peter 1:5 instructs us to add knowledge to our virtue, "For this very reason, make every effort to supplement your faith with virtue, and virtue with knowledge."

As you learned in the last chapter, virtue is a commitment to integrity and wholeness. Although virtue determines how to do what is right, your personal and marital decisions can only be virtuous when they are anchored in the knowledge of God's Word.

God does not want your marriage's faith and virtue to be relative concepts that ebb and flow with the social mores and temperament of the times. No, God expects your partnership to reflect an absolute truth that is centered on understanding His will and His way. In a culture bent on political correctness and situational morality, Peter's instruction to add knowledge to virtue affirms that it's imperative for a marriage to depend on God's Word as its compass.

This familiar passage in Hosea 4:6, which gives us insight on how important knowledge is to our Christian walk, can also be directly applied to marriage: "My people are destroyed for lack of knowledge; / because you have rejected knowledge, / I reject you from being a priest to me. / And since you have forgotten the law of your God, / I also will forget your children."

We are in dire need of . . . couples whose search for meaning, significance and purpose is grounded in scriptural principles.

Have you ever considered the implications of the lack of godly knowledge in your marriage? Think of it this way: God's Word is like a lighthouse for your marriage. When viewed in its proper context, the Bible helps you navigate through stormy situations in your relationship so you can steer clear of treacherous areas. When Scripture's instruction is ignored, however, couples lose perspective of to whom their marriage actually belongs. Rather than seeing it as belonging to God, they think it belongs to them. With this wayward perspective, they think they can do whatever they want with it.

However, as Hosea 4:6 suggests, the absence of an accurate biblical perspective always leads to destruction, including the erosion of your marriage. When you reject God's input into your marriage, the consequences extend beyond you to your children and generations to come.

It's no wonder then that patterns of divorce, adultery and broken homes so consistently pass from one generation to the next. Has your forsaking of God's laws led to His forgetting of your children? Scripture offers an excellent example of the impact of the father's sin on a child in the story of Manasseh, king of Judah, who is chronicled as doing evil in the sight of the Lord by following the detestable practices of pagans (see 2 Chron. 33:2). He invoked God's anger by building altars to false gods, sacrificing children, practicing witchcraft and other heinous acts. Manasseh's wickedness led to his captivity at the hands of the Assyrians.

Though Mannaseh later repented of his wickedness and sought to restore Judah to God, his son Amon never recovered from his father's transgressions. Upon succeeding his father as king of Judah, Scripture says that Amon also did evil in the Lord's eyes by sacrificing to the same idols his father had made years earlier (see 33:22–23).

Unlike his father, however, he refused to repent—which ultimately led to his assassination. The sad father-son story of Manasseh and Amon led a nation of people astray in their relationship with God.

It would be a mistake, however, to assume the generational impact of sin is limited to biblical times. The reality is that we see the struggles all around us, including in our marriages. For example, research has shown that children of divorce are themselves more likely to divorce.[1]

Another critical aspect of knowledge: We must consider the full context of Scripture rather than view verses in isolation. So many Christians zero in on specific biblical passages with blatant disregard for the full message the Lord leaves us in the Bible. The result is often a distortion of Scripture's true intent. Whether the topic is submissiveness, intimacy, attire or another relational point, Christians often damage the marital relationship by misrepresenting Scripture.

When adding the grace of knowledge to virtue, we must solicit God's wisdom to capture His heart for our relationship, rather than narrowly interpreting Scripture to serve judgment or attempt to moralize personal preference. Second Timothy 2:15 admonishes us to "do your best to present yourself to God as one approved, a worker who has no need to be ashamed, rightly handling the word of truth."

However, rather than seeking to rightly divide the Word of Truth as Timothy advocates, many Christian marriages have been scarred with distorted and harmful beliefs attributed to Scripture.

As the Christian church, we have allowed our marriages to slowly fall away from a union that glorifies God and replaced it with a union that we want to glorify us.

As a Christian community, we are in dire need of godly couples committed to pursuing a marriage centered on truth telling—couples whose search for meaning, significance and purpose is grounded in scriptural principles.

The role of Scripture in the Christian marriage is to encourage, not manipulate. God presents His Word to us and gives us, as spouses, a choice as to the extent to which we obey it. Unfortunately, too many Christians choose to selectively interpret Scripture in order to sell their own personal point of view, place themselves on some moral high ground or marginalize others who don't subscribe to their point of view. Rather than being the liberating document that God intended, too many Christians manipulate the Holy Bible to restrict others. God intends Scripture to break the chains of bondage in your marriage—not to be the chain.

The constant pursuit of marital mutuality is the challenge to which every married couple is called.

A Marriage of Mutuality

In 1998, God directed Dalia and me to move across the country from our home in Maryland to California, where I enrolled in the Marriage and Family Therapy (MFT) graduate program of Fuller Theological Seminary's School of Psychology. This was a daunting move that, at the time, felt like a major leap into the unknown and caused us to question whether we had heard God correctly.

The cost to enroll in Fuller's program was significant, and the weight of this financial reality was compounded by the fact that I had turned down a full scholarship to a comparable program at my alma mater (University of Maryland, College Park) which was a short commute from our home. Consequently, moving to California meant I'd have to work full-time while going to school in order to support our family.

Furthermore, going to Fuller meant we'd be thousands of miles from our family and friends. With two young children, financial uncertainty, and only a vague sense of what all of this ultimately meant, it was an anxious time for my family and me. Fortunately, we'd soon meet Jack and Judy Balswick, a couple unlike any other.

Soon after arriving on the Fuller campus, we newbies were invited to Jack and Judy's house for a meet and greet with faculty and both current and new students.

As senior professors at Fuller, the Balswicks are credited with establishing the MFT program as one of the premier, faith-based graduate programs approved by the American Association of Marriage and Family Therapists (AAMFT).

I wasn't sure what to expect when I met them, but I was totally unprepared for the level of authenticity, warmth and openness that they expressed to us as prospective students. It didn't take long for me to realize that God had indeed directed this transition.

Over the next three years, I would sit in classes they taught solo and as a couple. I would share with them my hopes and dreams of becoming an influencer for marriage. They became more than faculty members to me.

As a husband and wife team doing what I hoped my wife and I would one day do, they became our mentors. On one occasion, they even invited Dalia and me to attend a marriage retreat with them in order for us to observe them in action.

I can tell you many things about Jack and Judy. I could talk about the hundreds of articles, presentations and books that they've written. I could describe the collegial, nurturing yet professional, atmosphere they instilled in the MFT program and faculty.

I could tell you about the legion of marriage and family therapists and family-life educators that attribute their success to the Balswicks' tutelage. I could even tell you how much I blushed during the early weeks of their human sexuality course. But none of these things quite capture what Jack and Judy taught me about how knowledge adds to virtue in marriage, as noted in Second Peter 1:5. Through detailed exegesis of God's Word, Jack and Judy's impartation transformed my understanding of God's design for the husband-wife relationship by challenging me to objectively consider the apostle Paul's admonition to the church at Ephesus.

> Wives, submit to your own husbands, as to the Lord. For the husband is the head of the wife even as Christ is the head of the church, his body, and is himself its Savior. Now as the church submits to Christ, so also wives should submit in everything to their husbands.
>
> Husbands, love your wives, as Christ loved the church and gave himself up for her, that he might sanctify her, having cleansed her by the washing of water with the word, so that he might present the church to himself in splendor, without spot or wrinkle or any such thing, that she might be holy and without blemish. In the same way husbands should love their wives as their own bodies. He who loves his wife loves himself. For no one ever hated his own flesh, but nourishes and cherishes it, just as Christ does the church, because we are members of his body. "Therefore a man shall leave his father and mother and hold fast to his wife, and the two shall become one flesh." This mystery is profound, and I am saying that it refers to Christ and the church. However, let each one of you love his wife as himself, and let the wife see that she respects her husband. (Eph. 5:22–33)

It is important to note, however, that my education was not primarily an academic one. In my three years with Jack and Judy and other MFT professors, I observed a scriptural phenomenon that was entirely new to me—a marriage of mutuality. The Balswicks demonstrated how such mutuality demands an honesty and openness regarding all matters in order to make the best decisions for the good of the marriage and the family, rather than for the good of the individual. My life, marriage and ministry have never been the same.

I was raised in a fairly traditional Pentecostal church that held to highly stereotypical gender roles in marriage. This model tends to be quite patriarchal, with wives usually getting the "short end of the stick." Sermons and marital counseling, if they even exist, usually consist of men constantly reminding women that God has commanded them to submit to their husbands and that husbands are to be the head of their wives. Of course, these are indeed scriptural admonitions in Ephesians 5:22–23.

The problem, however, arises when the remainder of Ephesians 5 is ignored or marginalized. Little if any emphasis is placed on what it takes for husbands to actually show the same type of love for their wives that Christ showed for the church (see 5:25).

When you truly listen to the emotional needs of your spouse, you're able to respond from a place of sensitive acceptance.

Seldom are husbands challenged to love their wives as their own bodies as Paul taught (see 5:28). As so well-articulated by Dr. Eggerichs in his book *Love & Respect: The Love She Most Desires, The Respect He Desperately Needs*, true knowledge of God's design for marriage can only be gleaned by honoring both the love and respect components of the equation.[2]

The sin of disobedience introduced hierarchy and imbalance into the marriage, distorting the marital reciprocity of love and respect that God intended. But Christ's redemptive work intends to restore marriage to its original design marked by mutuality. The constant pursuit of marital mutuality is the challenge to which every married couple is called. Marital mutuality isn't easy, but it's what gives growth-minded couples that unfair advantage. The love and respect that Jack and Judy Balswick taught through academic and scriptural text was important given our graduate context—but it was their interpersonal relationship that felt magical.

Jack is a scholarly academic with a great sense of humor, and Judy is a nurturing clinician who never seems short on empathy; their personalities are as dissimilar as Dalia's and mine.

Yet when they taught as a team, their differences were complementary; and one thing was unmistakable—they valued each other's gifts. You could see this in the way they deferred to each other in their teaching style. You could hear it in the stories that they openly shared about the highs and lows in their own marriage journey.

Marriage's Love Triangle

Through word and deed, the Balswicks demonstrated the beauty of mutuality in marriage. I use the term "mutuality" often when working with couples. While some immediately get its implication, others struggle with its meaning in their daily interactions.

Through my experience with Jack and Judy, I began to understand that mutuality may be more easily conceptualized as an equilateral triangle, each side identical in length. In fact, I think of it as a love triangle—acceptance, agreement and affirmation. Each component is equally important for establishing a foundation of trust between spouses upon which a thriving marriage may emerge.

Acceptance

The first prong of mutuality in marriage is acceptance. Acceptance means respecting your spouse's inherent value, attentively listening to his or her perspective, and validating his or her needs and concerns. Acceptance is a basic human emotion that determines how secure your spouse feels in the marriage. Of course, the opposite of acceptance is rejection, which happens when a spouse's input is dismissed or marginalized.

Let me use an example to clarify how to demonstrate acceptance in marriage. My wife, like many women, places a high value on having a clean home. As a mom who also works outside the home, she often stresses about having insufficient time and energy to clean our home to her liking.

Over the years, I have taken a number of different positions on my wife's worry about our home's cleanliness. In the early days, I tried to convince her that she was making a big deal out of nothing. As someone who also tends to prefer a clean house, I thought the house was fine. As you might imagine, that opinion didn't go over too well with my wife.

Eventually, I became a little wiser and told the kids that we had to help Mom around the house. We each were assigned chores to perform every other week. My wife was appreciative. This worked for a while until the schedules got the best of us, at which time her anxiety began to rise again. After realizing how this was affecting her mood, I decided to surprise her and hire a housecleaner to come in once a month. I'm still amazed at how much this improves Dalia's state of mind.

In retrospect, I can see that my first response to Dalia's concern was rejection. That rejection was not just about having a clean house. Dalia felt that what was important to her was rejected. I had dismissed something that meant a lot to her. In this instance, I had failed to demonstrate the mutuality that Jack and Judy taught me. This story, however, also demonstrates the power of acceptance. When you truly listen to the emotional needs of your spouse, you're able to respond from a place of sensitive acceptance, which in turn strengthens the marital bond. In marriage, mutuality always begins with acceptance. Without it, the marital foundation erodes.

Agreement

In my efforts to strengthen marriages over the years, I have sought to remove what I see as a common stumbling block that trips many unsuspecting couples. They want to live in agreement. The husband wants the wife to agree with him. The wife wants the husband to agree with her. Many assume that if they cannot agree on any single meaningful point, their relationship is at risk.

The reality is that most couples know little about conflict resolution. Unfortunately, too many couples see conflict as a sign of marital distress, which in worst cases is interpreted as evidence that they should never have married. In most instances, nothing could be further from the truth.

Disagreement is not a sign of marital incompatibility; rather, it is better understood as the simple by-product of differing opinions and preferences. Disagreement is natural. Ironically, disagreement is actually required to build a thriving marriage. Disagreement, when handled well, holds the possibility to stretch you beyond your comfort zone or to see things in a different way. Disagreement pushes you to examine your motives and teaches humility.

Of course, when not well managed, disagreement may open a dark side that fuels self-centered and contemptuous attitudes and behaviors. For crisis couples, disagreement may feel like a tornado that tears through a town destroying everything in its path. Everything feels like a point of contention until the moment the couple calls it quits emotionally, and often legally. Handling disagreement well and keeping it from becoming an albatross requires that you separate the divisive issue from the spousal relationship itself. Let me explain.

Whether or not you and your spouse agree on an issue is a matter of personal preference. Your concern for your spouse, however, is not about preference. It's about covenant. Thriving couples distinguish the contentious issue from the relationship itself.

They are not the same thing. I would like to redefine agreement from being oriented around a particular issue to being mutually committed to a godly relationship. Think of agreement as a team of two aligned against an issue rather than a contentious issue splitting two feuding parties.

Growth-minded couples commit to being aligned allies, even when they disagree about an issue. And when things seem particularly unfair, remember that's the perfect opportunity to give a grace card that proves God is bigger than the disagreement.

Here is an excellent rule of thumb to help you live out mutuality in the daily routine of marriage. When faced with searching for agreement over contentious issues, think carefully about which spouse cares the most about this issue from an emotional point of view.

Agreement happens when the spouse who cares less defers to the spouse who is most emotionally invested in the decision. My wife and I have plenty of such decisions.

One example is making the bed in the mornings. During my growing up years, my mother insisted that our beds be made first thing in the morning. A failure to make your bed was just asking for trouble. From the time I was old enough to get in and out of the bed myself until the time I left home at the age of eighteen, I made sure my bed was made. For me, it was as routine as brushing my teeth in the morning. So I thought that the proper way to leave the bedroom in the morning was a kept bed. To do otherwise was to be sloppy and irresponsible. So imagine my surprise to learn that my wife did not place the same priority on making a bed.

For many years, this irked me and got under my skin. I wondered how she could be so irresponsible. And, for many years, I would let her know my displeasure—sometimes by creating minor arguments. We eventually agreed on a rule that the last person out of the bed would make it up.

Following the rule of thumb to defer to the person for whom the issue is more emotionally weighted, my wife has done a commendable job over the years accommodating my request. Unless she was extremely pressed for time, she usually made the bed. Of course, the reality is that there is no universal principle of bed-making etiquette that my wife was violating.

It simply wasn't as big a deal to her as it was to me, mostly because she grew up in a home as the eldest of six, with five younger brothers. Beds in her childhood home were always a mess.

Though our "rule" still officially stands, my perspective (and anxiety) has shifted. My wife is a hardworking woman. She does an outstanding job of taking care of the family and our home, particularly given that she balances working full-time outside the home, coleading the marriage ministry at our local church with me, and conducting our own marriage enrichment workshops. If I want our bed made up every morning, the least I can do is give her a break and do it myself. So that's exactly what I do.

My relationship with Dalia is way more important than the rule. Such is the foundational principle of agreement and conflict resolution in general. I like to give couples a simple way of thinking about agreement: "Agreement is choosing to stay close when the circumstances could pull you apart."

Affirmation

The third and most neglected leg of the mutuality triangle is affirmation. Affirmation is encouragement. Affirmation may feel easy during those times in your marriage when you and your spouse feel on top of the world, but what about the dark days? What does it take to affirm one another when, as in the case of Jack and Judy, your nine-year-old son is diagnosed with terminal bone cancer and dies within four months of that fatal diagnosis?

The emotional pain and turmoil accompanying the death of a young child shake a marriage to its very core. The vacuum cannot be filled or healed with well-intended condolences. As the Balswicks will attest, healing only comes through the Lord's strength, affirmation and the accrued trust of a mutual marriage that sustains your sanity as well as your marriage.

Why does affirmation help? Though we live in a society with such technological advances as smartphones, video chat and essentially twenty-four-hour accessibility, many of us live with a profound sense of disconnectedness, even in the most intimate of relationships like marriage.

These disconnected marriages have little foundation to stave off the DRAGONS when troubles arise. As Gary and Barb Rosberg highlight in *The 5 Love Needs of Men and Women*, encouragement is among the top five needs of husbands and wives.[3] More importantly, the Holy Scripture commands us, particularly in First Thessalonians 5:11, to embrace relationships and encourage one another daily. In this particular verse, Paul instructs the church to "encourage one another and build one another up."

Yet many of us feel that there are few, if any, people who really care about us. Psychotherapists, counselors, antidepressants and addictive behaviors are used to fill the relational void that far too many of us feel.

The love triangle is the way this intimacy develops with God and man.

The fact that this relational void is felt even in marriage is alarming. Of course, it stems from an almost pandemic degree of self-centeredness.

The call for affirmation is to demand something more. More specifically, it is encouraging your spouse to fully become the person God created him or her to be in every way—physically, psychologically and spiritually.

Affirmation is a mindset. I like to describe it as "encouragement mentality." Affirmation is supportive but also challenging. Affirmation is pulling the best of your spouse forward in private and in public, where appropriate. Affirmation is the encouraging language and supportive actions that communicate care and generate trust.

One of the common problems with affirmation in marriage is that well-meaning spouses seek to affirm using their own encouragement language rather than striving to understand their spouse's language of encouragement. How is your spouse encouraged?

Similar to the love languages popularized by Dr. Gary Chapman in his best-selling book *The 5 Love Languages: The Secret to Love That Lasts*, your feeling of affirmation depends on what encourages you.[4] It may be supportive words or gestures. It may be gratitude.

For some, like myself, it may be pushing us to the next level. Spouses should know their partners well enough that they understand what encourages and discourages them—and if in doubt, they need to ask.

Knowledge is ideally acquired in a community that is committed to pray, serve and challenge each other.

The problem occurs when spouses assume that the same thing that encourages them encourages their spouse. Usually, that is not the case. Frankly, spouses are often so consumed with their own concerns, they don't think about the importance of affirming a spouse.

Over time, this negligence erodes the trust in the relationship because everyone needs encouragement; and people naturally gravitate emotionally toward those with whom they feel affirmed. Thriving couples understand that affirmation is icing on the marriage cake because it creates emotional and physical intimacy.

We started this chapter talking about knowledge, the kind that is grounded in the central truth of Scripture. The message of Scripture is a marriage relationship aligned with Christ's relationship to the Christian church, with Jesus as the Bridegroom and the church as the bride. I have heard this scriptural reference my entire life, but I had seldom seen it modeled until I met Jack and Judy. The lessons I learned from them extend far beyond the textbooks, and their impact goes far beyond my graduate training.

Today, much of my work with couples, as well as my own identity as a husband, are a result of Jack and Judy's marriage of mutuality. With the benefit of hindsight, I know now that they influenced my pursuit of knowledge—not just the academic kind, but also the kind of knowledge that emerges when you are exactly at the place where God wants you.

I know now that the journey through acceptance, agreement and affirmation frames the level of growth and intimacy in marriage. This happens because the love triangle also outlines your spiritual intimacy with Christ.

Mutuality with Christ

Acceptance is the condition of our heart to receive Christ as our personal Savior. Agreement is the decision to align your walk with Scripture. Affirmation is that mandate as proclaimed in the first chapter of the book of Acts to be a witness for Him along life's journey. The message is simple. The love triangle is the way this intimacy develops with God and man.

The love triangle is the ultimate truth of God's Word, the greatest commandment in fact. Jesus phrases it this way in Matthew 22:37–39: "Love the Lord your God with all your heart and with all your soul and with all your mind. . . . Love your neighbor as yourself." These verses underline the core of knowledge because they focus on love as an act of giving—an offering.

I would be remiss not to put some emphasis on the relational command in this greatest commandment. Jesus equates love for neighbor with love for Him. At its most impactful, knowledge is about the community more than the individual. I took years to truly understand why my years in California, though difficult, were some of the best years of my life.

Jack and Judy had followed the Lord's leading to establish an academic program that was really a community marked by acceptance, agreement and affirmation. Amazingly, this couple had leveraged the strength of their own marriage to foster a culture of mutuality that permeated the program's entire matriculation. This community emphasis has been a core value for Jack and Judy since the beginning of their relationship more than fifty years ago.

For the Balswicks, knowledge is ideally acquired in a community that is committed to pray, serve and challenge each other to grow spiritually and emotionally through thick and thin. This communal perspective is a constant reminder that our marriages do not belong to us.

Our marriages belong to God. He desires that you give your marriage as an acceptable offering that points your neighbors to their Creator during their times of uncertainty, just as Jack and Judy have done for me.

Knowledge's Grace Card

I commit to the pursuit of godly knowledge as to how to best accept, agree and affirm God's full purpose for us as individuals and as a couple.

7

Negotiate Self-Control

Moderation in all things, especially moderation.

—Ralph Waldo Emerson

Couples often want to know the secret to a thriving marriage that stands the test of time. Conventional thought most commonly attributes it to good communication skills. Others suggest the key to a long marriage is mastering conflict resolution. Often you will hear couples talk about the importance of compatibility in a marriage. A few, usually newlyweds, believe that it's just about love. "Love conquers all," they say. Of course, many Christian couples believe that their shared faith should be enough. Without question, all of these factors share some degree of truth.

Communication skills allow the couple to really feel like they understand one another. Conflict resolution skills give the couple tools to navigate through areas of disagreement without significantly damaging the relationship. Having shared interests surely fosters a sense of emotional connection and makes it easier for them to spend quality time together. A common faith core definitely enhances the husband and wife's ability to march in the same direction.

However, in the many years I have worked with couples I am convinced that none of these factors is the primary driver of marriages with an unfair advantage. Rather, I've come to believe that the number one driver of a thriving marriage is contentment. Not the contentment that balks at growth, but the contentment that fits the *Merriam-Webster OnLine Dictionary*'s definition of "the state of being happy and satisfied."[2] Sounds quite simple, doesn't it?

Yet a survey by the Institute for American Values and Hampton University found that only 62 percent of American couples describe themselves as "very happy" in their marriage.[1] This percentage falls even more among certain ethnic subgroups.

Mustering the willpower to sustain such self-control is clearly a kingdom principle.

Happiness languishes among so many couples because their marriage lacks self-control or the ability to live in moderation. Many couples, especially those in First World countries, are accustomed to excess. We constantly strive for better jobs, bigger houses, nicer cars, newer clothes and more money. Don't get me wrong. Nothing is necessarily wrong with any of these pursuits. However, danger lies in prioritizing their importance above the pursuit of godliness.

Also, Western culture, in general, is addicted to excess; and we do our best to export that value for excess around the world. But when is enough enough? The apostle John admonishes that we should "not love the world or the things in the world" (1 John 2:15). In similar fashion, Peter encourages us "to abstain from the passions of the flesh, which wage war against your soul" (1 Pet. 2:11). So, what does it mean for a couple to live a life of moderation and self-control?

Growth-Minded Moderation

The clear message of the kingdom is to trust God's provision rather than the pursuit of more stuff of this world. Actually, Exodus 16:4 shows us a poignant example. God promises the Hebrew people that He will miraculously supply them with food each day in the form of manna from heaven. But there was one key stipulation.

The manna was only edible for that day. It would spoil and be inedible the following day. The message to the Hebrew nation—and to us—is that we must trust the Lord alone for our most basic provisions, our life's sustenance. The Lord makes His intention clear. The purpose is to test what we believe to be our life's source. Will it be God or man?

One of the ways Dalia and I gauge our own trust in God's provision is through the practice of tithing. During our twenty-seven years of marriage, we have consistently given back to God 10 percent of our earned income.

Tithing is a nonnegotiable habit for us because we believe that God will bless the remaining 90 percent to cover all of our needs and many of our wants. I admit that when I hear my friends talk about how much money they have amassed, I sometimes wonder if we might have more in our bank account had we not been tithing. At the same time, I believe that one can never put a price on obedience to God's instructions.

What financial or physical calamity did God protect us from because we are obedient to this instruction? Which job opportunities came our way because of our obedience to God? When my son was offered a full tuition and board scholarship to a major US college through the favor shown him by a friend, I can't help but wonder if it was connected to our trust in God's provision through tithing?

The reality is that we do not know. Given my theological worldview, I certainly do not suggest our behavior compelled God to act on our behalf. But I certainly believe that God is faithful in meeting the needs of those who place their trust in Him.

God asks you the exact same question in your marriage. Who will you trust: God or man? Couples bent on the pursuit of excess leave a trail of disappointment and wounds in their wake.

For some couples, financial ruin has resulted from a string of ill-advised businesses that have failed or from bankruptcies declared after overextending on mortgages.

Other couples are stuck in gambling, drug, pornography, food and other addictions arising from uninhibited lust of the flesh, lust of the eye and pride of life as John describes in First John 2:16: "For all that is in the world—the desires of the flesh and the desires of the eyes and pride of life—is not from the Father but is from the world."

Even religion can become a pursuit of excess if it stands in the way of truly understanding the love that God calls us to have for Him, our family and our neighbors. Regardless of its manifestation, a marriage of excess is doomed to physical and spiritual failure. If you and your spouse don't struggle with excesses of sex, money, cars, drugs and shopping, you might feel morally superior to those who do. But this is a trap.

Second Peter 1:6 pushes us to think more broadly about moderation by asking us if our knowledge of Scripture's truth is supplemented with self-control, which is not only a grace, but also a fruit of the Spirit (see Gal. 5:22-23).

When I consider this passage (2 Pet. 1:6) introspectively, I see my failings more clearly. I see the man whose marriage is perpetually strained by the excessive pursuit of that ever-elusive "success," which is so hard to quantify. I ask myself to soberly consider the toll that those long nights and weekends spent working to build a "platform of purpose" took on our marriage.

At its best, self-control is accepting our limitations and trusting in God's provision.

Yes, I try to be sensitive to my wife's concerns about the stress this pursuit has placed on her and on me—and, yes, I plan those date nights so that we can have some quality time together. But when I stare deeply at the man in the mirror, I know in my heart that my good intentions do not exonerate my attitude of excess. In my spirit, I sense the bigger truth reflected in our feature passage as well as the whole of Scripture.

This truth is that being growth-minded requires that we honestly yield our selfish desires, no matter how noble or egregious we believe them to be, to the truth of Scripture. We must maintain an attitude of moderation rather than excess in *all* matters. In this way, we add self-control to knowledge.

Graceful Self-Control

In chapter 5, I spoke about my trip to South Africa. I thoroughly enjoyed the frolicking waves of Cape Town's beaches, the history of Robben Island and the intrigue of Soweto, but I was most impacted by our three-hour trip through Langa Township. Langa Township, the oldest township in Cape Town, was established in 1923. Langa was one of the designated areas for black Africans during the pernicious apartheid reign and, as with all South African townships, is woefully underdeveloped.

Although I enjoyed my family's visit to Langa Township, I was starkly aware of the economic disparity between most people in this community and my own middle-class American lifestyle. I experience this same awareness each time I am privileged to glimpse at life in Third World countries such as Nicaragua and Panama.

God is more important than money, pleasure, work or anything else in life.

As I engage residents in these communities, I feel an overwhelming sense of injustice because of the depravity I see and the excess I experience back home. Yet these communities demonstrate a level of contentment and moderation, even if forced by the economic realities, that can be lessons for us all.

The instruction to add self-control to knowledge is a message of obedience and trust that spans socioeconomic strata. In many ways, Scripture teaches us many lessons on self-control, but none may be more pointed than that which is captured in the second chapter of Titus. Four times in this short chapter of only fifteen verses, we are called to live a life of self-control.

Older men are to show self-control (see Titus 2:2). Older women are to teach the younger women self-control, which of course means they must first demonstrate it (see 2:3–5). Younger men are to be self-controlled (see Titus 2:6). Mustering the willpower to sustain such self-control is clearly a kingdom principle. Paul summarizes it this way in Titus 2:11–12: "For the grace of God has appeared, bringing salvation for all people, training us to renounce ungodliness and worldly passions, and to live self-controlled, upright, and godly lives in the present age."

Again, we see grace as a central feature of kingdom living, or following Christ. Titus 2:11–12 illuminates how God's grace brings salvation. We understand well this cardinal aspect of the Christian faith. But I love the last part of the passage, namely, that God's grace trains us. What does it train us to do? It trains us to renounce ungodliness and worldliness, in other words the motivation for excess, and also trains us to live with self-control.

I like the way Pastor Rick Warren, author of *The Purpose Driven Life*, describes Christians with biblical self-control as demonstrating six behaviors: (1) mood mastery, (2) scrutiny of their words, (3) restraint in their reactions, (4) time management, (5) financial acumen and (6) health consciousness.

Balancing these requires a renewing of the mind that Paul describes in Romans 12:2: "Do not be conformed to this world, but be transformed by the renewal of your mind." Of course, we need more than mere willpower to renew our minds. Neither you nor I can sustain these biblical behaviors by ourselves. That is the irony. Ultimately, having self-control requires that we relinquish control of our lives to God.

As Jerry Bridges, author of *Holiness Day by Day: Transformational Thoughts for Your Spiritual Journey*, says, "Self-control is not control by oneself through one's own willpower but rather control of oneself through the power of the Holy Spirit."[3] At its best, self-control is accepting our limitations and trusting in God's provision. It is the exchange of an old self-sufficient attitude for a new grace-infused perspective. In marriage, self-control is a growth-minded act of grace established upon a foundational knowledge of God's Word.

Divine Provision

The clarion call for moderation reminds me of the resilient journey of Pernell and Diane Bradshaw. The Bradshaws have packed a lot of living into more than twenty-five years of marriage. When I met them, they had recently completed a book chronicling a turbulent period in their marriage when everything seemed to be falling apart. The story of how this well-respected, conservative Christian couple, seen by many as having a model marriage, made a series of poor and uncharacteristic decisions reads like a bad soap opera that even includes an extramarital affair and a crime spree.

Those familiar with the Bradshaw's passion for ministry, leadership and family would never expect how it was all sacrificed for self-centered lusts . . . and yet it was.

This chapter focuses on self-control, but this leg of Pernell and Diane's journey demonstrated anything but such restraint. Had the Bradshaw's story ended at that point in their marriage, it would have been a disturbing vignette of what happens when self-control is lost. It would have been a sad story of unfulfilled potential and betrayal.

Actually, the Bradshaw's story would have been a case study of the warning in Proverbs 25:28: "A man without self-control / is like a city broken into and left without walls." Without self-control, there are no boundaries to our human depravity.

Fortunately, the Bradshaws' story in its entirety is just the opposite. In fact, it is a story of incredible resilience and divine provision. God used this challenging time in their journey to chisel out a solid foundation of self-control that has sustained them through experiences that topple many marriages. One such example of self-control is the lengthy stint tthrough which the Bradshaws stayed unified and thrived as a couple when Pernell, who was an experienced professional and the primary income earner, was unable to find work in his field.

Despite the reality of their financial situation, Pernell and Diane's ability to moderate their lifestyle while maintaining a positive attitude was remarkable.

God brings light and provision to the dark and uncertain places if we stay faithful to Him.

Given my familiarity with their finances, I sometimes wondered, "How can they take that nice vacation?" and "How long will they be able to afford their home?" The most remarkable aspect of the Bradshaws' struggle was how they maintained a focus on helping and ministering to others even in the midst of their own uncertainty.

So many couples are waiting for everything to fall into place, which rarely happens. They erroneously believe that only when things line up for them, will they be able to focus on God's command to love Him and to love their neighbors. But Pernell and Diane's story taught me something quite profound.

I learned from watching the Bradshaws that a universal currency called "faith" is far more powerful than money. When a couple embodies this kind of faith, God turns the universe to meet their needs—and even many of their wants.

Listening to the Bradshaws' stories of God's miraculous provision through others who gave them vacations and other divine gifts, I thought of Psalm 24:1: "The earth is the LORD's and the fullness thereof, / the world and those who dwell therein." The message here is that when we embrace moderation and self-control, we make room for God to wield His control in our lives.

When we give in to excessive pursuits, we push our faith in God to the margins. In a way, we become our own gods, feeling as if we can provide for ourselves. In the book of Ecclesiastes, Solomon captured the result of this excessiveness best by calling it meaningless vanity, and saying that God is more important than money, pleasure, work or anything else in life.

Today, Pernell and Denise Bradshaw have taken their experiences of lack and plenty to form the foundation for a growing ministry. I cannot help but smile when I think about the transformation from their old life to their new one. I have had the opportunity to observe their ministry on several occasions.

One thing is clear above all else: The Bradshaw's ability to add self-control to knowledge not only sustained them as a couple during a difficult season, but is actually what gives credibility and sustenance to their ministry. Their story and ministry demonstrate how God brings light and provision to the dark and uncertain places if we stay faithful to Him, to one another and to the purpose to which He calls us as a couple.

Self-Control's Grace Card

I commit to a level of trust in God such that my life demonstrates an attitude of contentment with His provision for our marriage.

8

Commit to Persevere

By perseverance the snail reached the ark.

—Charles Spurgeon

Eight. That's the median number of years a divorced American couple's marriage lasted before they called it quits according to latest US Census Bureau data.[1] Such data seems to lend credence to the "seven-year itch," the psychological term suggesting that happiness in marriage declines around its seventh year.

Lest we think this is a phenomenon unique to American culture, let's take a look at marital longevity in ten cities around the world. Not that it's any consolation, but a US city doesn't receive credit for the shortest average marriage length.

That dubious distinction goes to Doha, Qatar with an unbelievable five and one-half years. Cape Town, London and Tokyo check in at a mere eleven years, followed by Mexico City, Sydney and New York City at twelve years. Paris and Ottawa are slightly better, where the average marriage lasts thirteen years. Rome then rounds out the top ten at a whopping eighteen years! Apparently, couples in Italy stay together longer than any other country that was evaluated.[2]

You do not need a research degree to analyze this data. Marital dissolution is a global phenomenon. As disturbing as these numbers are, especially for someone like me who is committed to helping marriage thrive for the long term, marriage longevity statistics will continue to decline in the United States and abroad. And the problem is even larger than these numbers, which focus explicitly on divorce, suggest.

In reality, many couples who stay married are also not committed to the growth of the marriage. They stay together for convenience, the children, the finances, social stigma or maybe just apathy. Regardless of the reason for "sticking it out," marriages suffer from failure to thrive. Couples are officially married, but they are living as though they are single.

Encouraged by the Holy Spirit, these couples embody the belief that weeping may endure for a night, but joy will come in the morning .

No matter how you explain this commitment deficit in marriage, it points to a lack of long-term investment in the relationship that God intended for a lifetime. God's ideal plan for you and your family does not include separation—legally or emotionally. If you truly grasp this fact, you will receive a richer perspective on the next lesson in our feature passage, which instructs us to supplement self-control with steadfastness.

"For this very reason, make every effort to supplement your faith with virtue, and virtue with knowledge, and knowledge with self-control, *and self-control with steadfastness*, and steadfastness with godliness, and godliness with brotherly affection, and brotherly affection with love" (2 Pet. 1:5–7). Some translations use the word "perseverance" rather than "steadfastness." Because "perseverance" is more commonly used in contemporary vernacular, we will adopt that term.

Perseverance is defined as "steady persistence in a course of action, a purpose, a state, etc., especially in spite of difficulties, obstacles, or discouragement."[3]

In the last chapter, we dissected what it means to live with self-control and moderation rather than succumbing to the pressure of excess. For most of us this is not an easy endeavor in marriage. Though we often start with the best of intentions, our resolve wanes. We fall back into familiar patterns that leave our faith in God and our marriage adrift.

When Peter instructs us to add perseverance to self-control, I believe the Holy Spirit is speaking directly to this human tendency to regress to self-centeredness rather than maintaining a focus on what God is doing. Most people have the willpower for self-control for a short period of time.

However, Peter's instruction challenges us to persevere in making the daily choices that sustain self-control. The operative phrase here is "daily choices."

Daily Affirmation

A common misnomer about what makes a marriage thrive is that the couple has simply committed to a marriage that lasts a lifetime. Of course, this is true at some level, but it is not the central truth.

The key to marital satisfaction is not in the commitment that one makes to stay married until death. Most of us know couples who do not like each other very much but lack the will to leave each other. That is not a thriving marriage. Rather, the happiest marriages are ones in which spouses commit to making daily choices to affirm each other. You might recall that I spoke about the power of affirmation in chapter 6. Ask any couple whose marriage has grown for twenty, forty or sixty years, and you will hear a consistent theme.

They persisted in making daily decisions of affirmation that built safety and trust. Growth-minded marriages refuse to take *today* for granted. They realize that a successful marriage takes a lifetime commitment to building their marriage according to God's blueprint.

A "right relationship" is a relationship that is redemptive.

We can use home construction as an example here. A home-builder depends on a blueprint to guide his action on every detail of a home—from its foundation to its framing to its finishing. He cannot simply commit to building a house.

That's a great aspiration, but what gives this ambition substance is the commitment to complete each step with integrity, so the owners are pleased with the completed project. Perseverance is critical to marriage because the aspiration for a great marriage is good, but it's not enough.

Thriving couples persevere in the level of detailed attention to God's blueprint (knowledge), holding them accountable (self-control) for producing a marriage that is ultimately pleasing to Him. To whom does your marriage belong? If you say, "my marriage belongs to God," then He is the owner.

We all must challenge ourselves to consider how pleased the owner of our marriage is with the product we produce. You cannot answer this question by thinking about what your marriage will be like twenty or thirty years from now.

Rather, you first decide to demonstrate personal integrity in your marriage. Then, you decide that you will do that every day for the rest of your married life. I believe this is what it means to supplement self-control with perseverance.

If we look more closely at the definition of perseverance, we see the challenge. To persevere is to continue in spite of difficulties, obstacles and discouragement. The daily commitment to a growth-minded marriage does not happen on a proverbial bed of roses.

Thriving marriages do not exist only for couples who were lucky enough to avoid life's potholes. In fact, the opposite is true. Extraordinary marriages exist because the fires of life have forged a bond, rather than created a wedge, between them. Marital spats, wayward children, financial pressures, in-law intrusions and health scares are just a few of the circumstances through which these couples persevere.

How do they do it? They find it within themselves to embrace their unfair advantage and stay connected to a God who promises them that He will not put more on them than they can bear. Encouraged by the Holy Spirit, these couples embody the belief that weeping may endure for a night, but joy will come in the morning (see Ps. 30:5).

Perseverance of the Saints

We have been looking at the importance of perseverance specifically in the context of marriage. But perseverance more broadly has long been at the center of biblical theology. In fact, Calvinism and Reformed theology tout "perseverance of the saints" as one of their five key precepts, which captures the importance of remaining steadfast and sure in our faith without succumbing to sin. Perseverance allowed the apostle Paul to say, "I have fought the good fight, I have finished the race, I have kept the faith" (2 Tim. 4:7). Paul does not attribute this perseverance to anything of his own nature. Rather, he acknowledges that solely through God's grace within him is perseverance even possible.

In fact, the centrality of grace is clear in the theological definition of perseverance—"continuance in a state of grace to the end, leading to eternal salvation."[4] I love that definition because it acknowledges the source of our strength. In ourselves, we have no capacity to stay in right relationship with God, and our inability to stay true to God leaves us unable to stay in right relationship with our spouse. Our sinfulness inevitably leaves us falling short of God's standard on all counts.

When I say staying in "right relationship" with your spouse, I mean more than getting along, achieving shared goals and communicating well. These are noteworthy accomplishments for any marriage, but a "right relationship" is a relationship that is redemptive, for us as individuals, as couples and as positive influences on our society. Such is the power of spousal redemption.

It is an outgrowth of Christ's redemptive work. That is the lesson that our next marriage exemplar, Albert and Debbie Blackstock, will teach us. On every level, redemption is the means by which grace is possible.

The Redemptive Power of Perseverance

Albert and Debbie Blackstock personify the perseverance of which Scripture speaks. With more than three decades of marriage behind them, you might think that they would have their marriage set on cruise control.

After all, they have been students and teachers of marriage enrichment for many years. They have read dozens of marriage self-help books and have been trained in several marriage empowerment tools. They have personally counseled couples and have led many groups of engaged and married couples through formal curricula.

But, this dedication to marriages has not gone unchallenged. In fact, it never does. The Enemy recognizes the threat that the Blackstocks and those with their zeal pose to his nefarious agenda. The more impactful a marriage becomes, the more interruptions the Enemy will throw its way.

The blood of Christ perseveres, which in turn empowers us to persevere.

For the Blackstocks, this meant facing serious health and financial challenges. Albert's employment as the chief financial officer of a large nonprofit was strained as the organization dealt with major financial crises. At the same time, Debbie's employer released her after many years of service.

But the most emotionally devastating blow was the strained relationship with their eldest daughter, who, as a teenager, rejected the moral and faith lessons that she had been taught over the years.

The relationship soured to the point where the Blackstocks made the difficult decision of telling their daughter to leave the home. Their daughter became a single mother before completing her senior year of high school.

As most parents would be, the Blackstocks were devastated, and they struggled with their decision. Each of these incidences, and the cumulative weight of them all, placed an enormous strain on the Blackstocks' marriage. Despite the certainty of their faith during this dark period, they recount times when they simply felt God was silent.

Yet, remarkably, they managed to thrive, and even to grow closer in the process. How did they do it? How does a couple persevere when facing life's most difficult decisions—especially when the welfare of their children is involved, and they disagree about the best way to proceed? I posed that very question to Albert during one of our many discussions. His answer was profound in its simplicity. "Grace," he responded.

For the Blackstocks, grace is more than a theoretical component of their faith. Grace is the lifeline that kept their marriage centered on God even in the midst of a maelstrom. Grace is the lubricant that smoothed the path for forgiveness to flow throughout their family.

Albert and Debbie are convinced that the tremendous disappointment they felt pressed them into a space of faith, even amid the tears. The Blackstocks' journey brings the Romans 5:3 passage to life, "We rejoice in our sufferings, knowing that suffering produces endurance"—or perseverance.

A glimpse at the Blackstocks' lives today proves the truth of this Scripture. Today, the Blackstocks' relationship with their estranged daughter has been healed because they persevered. They credit this to God's revelation to them that their daughter belongs to Him—not them.

Consequently, they showed their daughter the same love that God shows them. Their perseverance was emboldened by this revelation, combined with the gracious support of a community of trusted friends who had endured similar familial challenges. The result has been a relational miracle.

Now, because they refused to quit, the Blackstocks have a beautiful granddaughter who is one of their life's joys. They continue to minister a message of grace to couples through life's peaks and valleys. Couples seek their counsel not only because they are authentic, but also because they can patiently wait for a godly transformation.

The Blackstocks own difficulties have chiseled within them an understanding of an unfair advantage that only comes when couples embody God's grace through difficulties, refusing to submit to the DRAGONS. Such is the power of perseverance.

Thankfully, we serve a risen Christ whose blood covers all of our shortcomings. The blood of Christ perseveres, which in turn empowers us to persevere. Without question, difficulties will arise because you have an Adversary who seeks to diminish your godly inheritance.

But, you also have a Comforter who is greater than the Force of Darkness. The salvation of your soul and your marriage hinge on two factors: (1) your persistent submission to the Holy Spirit and (2) acceptance of God's grace when missteps happen.

Perseverance's Grace Card

I commit the best part of me to keeping our marriage moving toward God and, as a redemptive spouse, modeling Christ who covers all our needs.

9

Embrace a Godly Lifestyle

Every day that we're not practicing godliness we're being conformed to the world of ungodliness around us.

—Jerry Bridges
The Fruitful Life

When the Lord first gave me Second Peter 1:3-11 as an encouragement for couples, I didn't take too long to understand it—at least most of it. I could see exactly how each encouragement progressively built upon the previous one, until I came to "godliness." Then I just scratched my head. "Why would I talk about godliness specifically?"

I wondered quizzically, "Hasn't each step to the unfair advantage been about godliness?" These questions led to a deeper examination of the apostle Peter's intention in this passage. The word transliterated as "godliness" is from the Greek *eusebeia*.

Only as I understood the meaning of *eusebeia* (the *Matthew Henry Commentary on the Whole Bible* describes it as adopting a lifestyle that is respectful and reverential toward God[1]), did I realize the depth of the next grace.

The key idea here is that godliness is a "lifestyle" defined by the way it respects God. Theologian Ray Stedman describes godliness as a "continual awareness of God's presence affecting and governing every aspect of life."[2]

By adding godliness to perseverance, Peter reminds us that our endurance works patience, which builds the necessary character to sustain a God-centered lifestyle. Godliness is a commitment to a lifestyle that engages you holistically—body, mind and spirit. A godly lifestyle is about relationship with God rather than about following prescribed rules.

A rule-based faith is emblematic of a fixed-minded nature and will never please God for one simple reason—our sinful nature prevents us from satisfying all the rules necessary to be in right relationship with God.

Godliness is an act of reconciliation that starts individually but always has communal impact.

Only through the cleansing blood of Christ can we stay in relationship with the Father despite the trail of broken rules along the way. As we have seen with other behaviors, a lifestyle of godliness is only possible through a grace-filled relationship.

Irreconcilable Differences

Here is a riddle for you: How can a man and a woman get married twice in a thirteen-year period but only have one spouse during that time? Is it obvious? This is the journey of Clint and Penny Bragg.

In 1989, they married each other for the first time in the presence of jubilant family and friends. On the surface, Clint and Penny seemed to be poster children for a young, Christian marriage. As committed Christians who were active church members, they could check the boxes that most people use to measure marriage potential.

Things went fairly well for the first year of marriage. By the second year, however, their relationship began to seriously break down when their huge personality differences began getting the best of them. What began as minor irritations mushroomed into acrimonious conflicts; and, as the Braggs will tell you, they were both too proud to abandon the facade of a "happy marriage" to trusted people who could help them.

Tensions mounted and, shortly before their second anniversary, only one option seemed plausible to Penny. She decided to pack a few things in a suitcase and walk out on Clint and their fledgling marriage. The last time Clint and Penny saw each other for eleven long years was during the notarization of their divorce papers, which cited "irreconcilable differences have caused the permanent breakdown of our marriage."

If the story ended there, Clint and Penny would just be another disappointing statistic of a marriage that ended before it even really started. "Irreconcilable differences" is what they and other self-centered couples call their preference to idolize their own wants over God's desire for them.

The truth is that divorce has nothing to do with irreconcilable differences and everything to do with irreconcilable spirits. Clint and Penny, like so many other couples, failed to subject their own spirits or wills to the leading of the Holy Spirit.

To clarify, in most instances, "irreconcilable differences" is a statement of a couple's spiritual relationship with God more than a prognosis of their marital relationship. The Braggs' unwillingness to allow the Holy Spirit to operate in their marriage created an irreconcilable spirit where the only plausible option appeared to be an escape hatch—marital dissolution.

Focusing on Penny's abandonment and pointing a blaming finger in her direction would be easy, but the truth is much deeper. As evidence of the stubborn nature of an irreconcilable spirit, Clint had already gone through two divorces prior to meeting Penny.

Thus, as I stated above, in most instances, a declaration of irreconcilable differences is more a statement regarding spiritual maturity than a statement of relational health.

Sadly, so many couples continue to labor through marriage with an irreconcilable spirit. They think the problem lies with their spouse.

Like an auctioneer, they can effortlessly rattle off a list of their spouse's mistakes, indiscretions and personality challenges.

Though most husbands and wives do have shortcomings—as we all do—I would like to suggest that 20 percent of marital difficulties stem from their attitude and behavior differences.

I believe that 80 percent of marital difficulties, therefore, must be attributed to something else, namely, an irreconcilable spirit that creates space for the DRAGONS to flourish.

For eleven long years, Clint and Penny had absolutely no contact with one another. Yet, neither one of them remarried. What Clint and Penny did not know was that they were both deliberately engaged in an emotional and spiritual healing process during this period. They each connected with God anew.

Their irreconcilable spirits dissipated and were replaced by *eusebeia*—a lifestyle that was sensitive to and respectful of God's presence. With space to hear God, Penny (who had walked out on her marriage eleven years earlier) penned a letter of apology to Clint. After a period of reconnection, forgiveness and reconciliation, Clint and Penny again met at the altar and remarried on August 17, 2002.

Clint and Penny's miraculous journey of two marriages has taught me a lot about the importance of authentic *eusebeia* or "godliness" in marriage.

Your marriage's unfair advantage is particularly poised to emerge when your own history is blemished by an irreconcilable spirit.

In their first marriage, Clint and Penny succumbed to that aforementioned "appearance of godliness" (2 Tim. 3:1–5). When Paul uses the word "godliness" in this Scripture, he qualifies it as a mere shell of what God intends. The "appearance of godliness" Paul refers to is religion without God's presence. It is a mirage of the marriage that God ordained. This godless religiosity leads to a lifestyle devoid of the Holy Spirit's power.

Reconcilable Differences

Despite their Christian backgrounds, Clint and Penny's irreconcilable spirits left them separate from Christ's true power and ignorant of the benefits of Christian membership. Their powerless marriage, like Clint's previous marriages, then crumbled under the strain.

That feeling of powerlessness prevailed until after the divorce, when counseling and an authentic connection with Christ empowered them to heal their emotional and psychological wounds. Scripture's admonition to incorporate godly reverence into the faith-building process is recognition that we continually need the blood of Christ to reconcile us back to the Father. There is a difference between God's ideal for you and where you are today. There is a difference between where your marriage is today and where God intends it to grow. As sinners, "all have sinned and fall short of the glory of God" (Rom. 3:23), but that difference is reconcilable as you demonstrate godliness.

Similarly, those differences in personality and preference between you and your spouse are also reconcilable. Those differences are your strength as a couple because they have the potential to shape you into the person and the couple God designed.

As you allow these differences to shape your marriage into "a Designer's original," you model a path that helps other couples reconcile their own differences with each other and with God. In other words, your experience of reconciliation is a gift that reconciles others. Godliness is an act of reconciliation that starts individually but always has communal impact.

Penny did not realize the impact her apology letter to Clint would have on couples across the world. In 2004, just two years after remarrying, Clint and Penny Bragg formed Inverse Ministries with the mission to "reconcile marriages across the nation . . . reclaiming the territory of marriage and family for God."[3] Twice a year Clint and Penny, known as marriage missionaries, embark upon forty- and twenty-one-day-missionary journeys that take them across the country to help couples heal their relationship with God and with each other.

In 2015 Clint and Penny published a book, *Marriage on the Mend,* that chronicles their amazing testimony of godliness.[4] But the Braggs' influence on the kingdom of God extends far beyond this book's 248 pages. Some will ask why I would feature the story of a couple with multiple divorces in their history as an exemplar of godliness. In reality, I hope this question is posed to me. The Braggs' story, like so many others, is an authentic demonstration of how God repeatedly redeems our failures. Your marriage's unfair advantage is particularly poised to emerge when your own history is blemished by an irreconcilable spirit.

Clint and Penny have transformed their failures into a resolute faith and in so doing have added godliness to perseverance. When they are in your presence, you feel the authentic compassion, safety and hopefulness within the depths of your spirit. Their message for crisis couples is simple, "There is no crisis that a couple committed to godliness cannot reconcile."[5]

Such godliness was the source of their strength a few years ago, when Penny's beloved brother inexplicably ended his own life and left his family reeling in grief and struggling to adapt to a new normal.

With their experiences, the Braggs will be the last ones to tell you that the path of godliness is easily traversed. They would be the first to tell you, however, that the pursuit of godliness is worth every ounce of effort that you invest. Earlier, I posed the riddle, "How, in a thirteen-year period, can a man and a woman get married twice but only have one spouse during that same period?"

Now that you've heard Clint and Penny's miraculous story from irreconcilable to reconcilable differences, you can see that the best answer to this riddle is one word, "Grace."

Godliness' Grace Card

I commit to a lifestyle in which I expect our difficulties to shape our marriage into a vessel of honor and an altar of worship to God.

10

Serve with Mutual Affection

A friend is someone who knows the song in your heart and can sing it back to you when you have forgotten the words.

—Unknown

Over these chapters, my prayer is that you have gained a keener sense of who God desires for you to become in your Christian walk and your marriage. The Holy Spirit's operation within you is to transform who you are as a Christian, which in turn renews your thinking about who you are as a spouse.

This is my personal story. Even after speaking to hundreds of couples and writing thousands of words on marriage, my mind must still be renewed daily in my interaction with my wife. When I get so consumed with elevating my priorities over God's, I stumble in marriage. I speak to my wife in a belittling tone. I judge her actions unfairly. My listening and communication skills deteriorate. When this spiral is in full swing, I am far removed from showing the godliness that we talked about in the last chapter.

In chapter 1, I described how my spirit was convicted when Dalia said to me in those early years of marriage, "I love you, but I don't like you very much." It felt like a slap in the face.

Actually, it was my wake-up call. My wife loved me because she took a vow to God to do so. But the "like factor"—or let's call it the "friendship of marriage"—was missing.

Despite being a married woman, Dalia felt alone because the best friend she thought she had married was anything but that. I felt guilty and ashamed.

Arguably, friendship (or the lack thereof) may be the best predictor of relational happiness and longevity. Yet the sad reality is that friendship is missing in many marriages, as it was in mine. Recent research in the *Journal of Social and Personal Relationships* shows that the friendship aspect of a romantic relationship is a strong predictor of love, sexual gratification and romantic commitment.

Without question, I believe the number one challenge of marriage is to acquire and sustain best friends status.

Relatedly, the research demonstrates that friendship is a protective barrier against dissolution of the relationship. Even more interesting is the fact that these benefits come specifically from valuing the friendship more than any other relational aspect (e.g., sexual intimacy).[1] This is not an isolated study.

Two researchers at the University of British Columbia's Vancouver School of Economics found that life satisfaction and well-being are about twice as prevalent for those whose spouse is also their best friend.[2] How's that for an unfair advantage?

I did not need research studies back then to tell me that something had to change in me if my marriage was to please

God—which has always been my stated goal. I felt it to my core. I needed to become more than Dalia's husband, more than a faithful sexual partner, more than a paycheck and more than a father to her children.

Yes, each of these is an important aspect of marriage, but one crucial element was missing—friendship. My wife, and every other wife and husband, needs a spouse who is a friend.

Best Friends Forever

Marriages are struggling because each spouse sees other roles they serve as more important than the best friend role. This is one of the great deceptions of marriage. The logic, however, is quite simple. What nearly all spouses want most from a marriage is to feel genuinely accepted—loved for who they are. When spouses feel accepted, they feel loved.

What does being married to your best friend mean? Best friends take personal responsibility for each other's emotional state. Best friends have each other's best interest at heart. Best friends communicate, even choosing to share the hard things. Best friends implicitly trust each other and give each other the benefit of the doubt.

Being best friends cannot be decreed by a pastor or certified by the state. Best friends status is first earned and then maintained at a personal cost. Without question, I believe the number one challenge of marriage is to acquire and sustain best friends status.

Suggesting that a married couple lacks best friends status may sound a little strange or maybe even off-putting. The results, however, speak for themselves. Best friends don't divorce one another or consistently prioritize their own needs over the needs of the other. Best friends don't stop communicating without regard for the impact on the other. Best friends don't dismiss each other's feelings. Yet these relational hang-ups are what I constantly hear from married Christian couples who are teetering on the brink of helplessness on how to salvage their marriage. Even couples who are not in crisis fail to see how their marital satisfaction is hampered by the lack of friendship in the relationship.

Psychologist John Gottman of the University of Washington confirms, "The only way to change marriage for the better is to improve the quality of friendship between a husband and wife and to help them deal with disagreements differently."[3]

That contemporary research validates the importance of friendship, especially in marriage, is good; the Bible also has long extolled friendship's benefits.

John 15:13 captures the sacrifice involved in true friendship: "Greater love has no one than this, that someone lay down his life for his friends." Authentic friendship at its purest form is an act of sacrifice—sometimes even the ultimate sacrifice as shown to us by Christ.

The Fruit of Friendship

Our feature passage in Second Peter 1:7 instructs us to add brotherly affection (some translations say "mutual affection") to the godly lifestyle that was discussed in the last chapter. According to First John 4:8, God is love and anyone without love lacks relationship with God.

We cannot love God and hate our neighbor. Stated another way, we cannot live out our kingdom purpose to love without having a heart for our neighbor.

After all, loving God and loving our neighbor are the greatest commandments (see Matt. 22:37–39).

I am personally committed to living out the kingdom principle of showing brotherly kindness, or mutual affection. But here is the challenge, not only for me but for every person of faith: *It is impossible to demonstrate this type of loving friendship outside the home while failing at it inside the home.* Far too many Christians, even pastors, want to minister to the spiritual and material needs of their neighbors without first meeting the needs of their families.

How can the majority of pastors report that they don't have a good marriage? How can 50 percent of pastors' marriages end in divorce?

This irony might explain the results of a Gallup poll indicating that only 42 percent of Americans have confidence in the Christian church or other organized religion. According to Gallup, "Americans have less confidence in organized religion today than ever measured before—a sign that the church could be 'losing its footing as a pillar of moral leadership in the nation's culture.'"[4]

Godliness is more than a self-help program. Heeding the instruction to supplement godliness with mutual affection is a call to spread what God is doing within you to the people that God is placing around you—these are your brethren.

Country music superstar Reba McEntire's classic 1983 song may capture it best, "Love isn't love 'til you give it away."[5] Until we become more proficient in giving love away in our homes, we will always struggle to take our godliness to a culture in need of God's Word made flesh.

The Face of Friendship: Michael and Denise Murray

God brought people like Michael and Denise Murray into my life to help me see what mutual affection in marriage looks like. (Honestly, this wasn't something that I had witnessed during much of my life.) I first met the Murrays in 1998 when I flew to Pasadena, California prior to entering the Marriage and Family Therapy graduate program at Fuller Theological Seminary. I was to unpack my family's furnishings from a freight trailer into the two-bedroom apartment that would be our home for the next three years. I had so many questions about what this seminary experience would be like in general.

But a more immediate question was "How am I going to move all of the boxes and furniture into a second-story apartment without an elevator?" The community coordinator had assured me that people would be there to help me, but the details of who, how and when were lacking. So, as I stared at the trailer full of our belongings when it arrived at the apartment complex, I could only hope that someone would come to my aid.

Sure enough, after a welcome dinner that evening, a gracious community pitched in to move my family's belongings into the seminary apartment.

Many people rallied to help with the move, but Michael Murray stayed behind to help me set things up. I'm not sure how long he hung in there with me that night. I do know that Michael's presence with me at a time of uncertainty and need left an indelible impression that's stayed with me for more than seventeen years.

I returned to Pasadena a few weeks later to officially begin this new season of life with Dalia and the kids, and Michael and his wife Denise quickly became our best friends.

Dalia and Denise prayed together. Denise was a trusted friend with our then nine-month-old daughter who didn't take to unfamiliar faces very quickly. Michael, also a first-year seminary student, and I became late night study partners at a local coffee house. Denise and Michael defined what it meant to demonstrate brotherly kindness to me and my family during a time when I was spread quite thin with full-time work and full-time school.

When I think about a couple that adds mutual affection to godliness, the Murrays immediately come to mind. When we lived in the same community with the Murrays all those years ago, we spent a lot of time with them at dinner, hanging out at the beach or a local park, or engrossed in some deep conversation in our homes.

We are in dire need of marriages whose light shines bright enough to bless them.

Dalia and I are quite different from the Murrays. We are a number of years older. We are African-American and they are Caucasian. We have biological children; they do not. We come from very different Christian traditions. We were raised in Apostolic churches (the *Apostolic* Church is a denomination that came from the Pentecostal movement), and they come from the Southern Baptist tradition. We hail from the East Coast and they are native Midwesterners. I could go on, but you get the point.

There were plenty of reasons that the Arnolds and the Murrays wouldn't be best friends; but during a critical season in both of our lives, and probably our marriages, we were just that.

The more remarkable point, however, is that both then and now Michael and Denise Murray have shown the uncanny ability to develop these same deep and meaningful relationships with many others—often people as dissimilar from them as Dalia and I were. As I think about this relational gift the Murrays have developed,

I am convinced that it stems from the mutual affection that they first show toward each other. During my early years of knowing Michael and Denise, I observed a number of things that affirmed this mutual consideration.

When we would go out for dinner or dessert, I often wondered why they would sometimes order one item and share it. I soon learned that this theme of sharing was evident in all the significant aspects of their marriage. I observed the way they shared in making major life decisions—both expecting to fully understand the other's perspective.

For example, we watched them rally around one another emotionally, spiritually and financially to meet their individual academic goals as Denise pursued a nursing degree followed by Michael's second graduate degree—a period which they deemed among the most difficult in their marriage, now in its twenty-third year.

Scripture instructs us to supplement godliness with mutual affection. Michael and Denise help us to understand how a thriving marriage embodies friendship and is characterized by the authentic sharing of time, resources and dreams with one another.

However, the ultimate beauty of their mutual affection lies in the way their strength and synergy as a couple radiate out to their family and their community.

I am reminded of the time when they brought Michael's teenage nephew from their home state of Michigan to live with them in California. He was drifting from his Christian roots; so they removed him from some negative influencers in his life, and they used this time to help him develop a firmer faith foundation and some important life skills.

Though this gesture saved their nephew in many ways, it put a tremendous strain on the Murrays' marriage.

Despite the challenge of raising their nephew during a transitional period in their own lives, they refused to let it diminish the brotherly kindness they showed to their community. Whether befriending a family like mine, working with the homeless on Los Angeles' Skid Row or encouraging a local youth group, they consistently demonstrated brotherly kindness.

I will always remember another such display of this sharing when they jointly decided to open their apartment, and their hearts, to an African-American teenager who had been a foster child of another couple in the community. They essentially became informal adoptive parents to this teenager who went on to live with them for several years.

When I think of what it means to be "the church" in our culture, the Murrays' marriage immediately comes to mind. Matthew 5:15 provides excellent imagery about sharing brotherly kindness: "Nor do people light a lamp and put it under a basket, but on a stand, and it gives light to all in the house."

In a culture that struggles to sustain deep and meaningful relationships in marriage and beyond, we are in dire need of marriages whose light shines bright enough to bless them and graciously serve everyone else in their path.

Mutual Affection's Grace Card

I commit to be your best friend who prioritizes your needs, advocates for your godly desires and challenges you to experience the best God has to offer.

11

Imitate Unfailing Love

I believe that unarmed truth and unconditional love will have the final word in reality. This is why right, temporarily defeated, is stronger than evil triumphant.

—Martin Luther King Jr.

In the English language, the word "love" is used to convey an array of relationships. One can love one's cat, job, child, spouse and God. We use the same word, "love," to express each of these, but hardly anyone would equate all of these relationships. The Greek language, in which New Testament Scripture is written, differentiates the types of love.

There is *philia*, which is brotherly love, the considerate friendship described in the last chapter on mutual affection. Then there is *storge*, which is a familial love that you may share with your siblings or your children. The third type of love is *eros*, which is a romantic love relationship commonly shared between husband and wife. Finally, there is *agape*, which is the Greek word for love at its ultimate self-sacrificing manifestation.

Agape, signified by God's sacrifice of His son, Jesus Christ, is the love that God has for you and me. Agape is an ultimate expression of love that always requires a commitment to make the ultimate sacrifice. Anything less is not agape. Agape sounds lofty and spiritual—maybe even sometimes outside our human capacity. Yet the apostle Paul tells us otherwise when he encourages us to "be imitators of God, as beloved children. And walk in love, as Christ loved us and gave himself up for us, a fragrant offering and sacrifice to God" (Eph. 5:1–2).

Ephesians was discussed in an earlier chapter, in which Paul informs husbands that their love for their wives should imitate Christ's love for the church (see 5:25). In this context, Paul insists that wives should imitate this love through submission (see 5:22).

Sincere faith is the belief that your marriage is a gift from God.

This idea of "submission" is an important one, but not just for the wife. The directive to imitate Christ's love through mutual submission (see 5:21) to one another is really the central feature of Paul's instruction to married couples.

Unfailing Love

When I think about agape love in marriage, I immediately go to one of Paul's most quoted chapters about love. Many, in fact, refer to First Corinthians 13 as Paul's "Love Chapter."

However, I just want to focus on a single passage from that amazing chapter. "Love never ends. As for prophecies, they will pass away; as for tongues, they will cease; as for knowledge, it will pass away" (13:8). We can easily move through this verse too quickly and miss it's key message that only love survives to the end—into eternity, in fact. Gifts, even the spiritual ones like prophecy, tongues and godly knowledge which we tend to prioritize in church, will pass away. When they do, love remains.

Love never fails. That, of course, is because God is love and He never fails. I am struck by the power of those three words: "Love never fails." Of course, that's how God loves us, but how can I as a husband, with all of my shortcomings, obediently demonstrate a "love that never fails" to my wife? Is that too tall an order for any husband when faced with a wife whose point of view is often different on various issues, from money to parenting to intimacy needs? The answer of course is "No."

God would not give us the instruction to show never-ending love unless we had the ability to obey. The real question is: How do we faithfully demonstrate the type of love that never fails?

Unending love must come from God. Any attempt to satisfy this love edict from your own human ability will prove insufficient. We may love during the good times. We may even love for a while during difficult seasons.

Unending love, however, only flows from a divine source—because that well never runs dry. Please take some time to reflect on this idea. Think of all the people within your sphere of influence to whom you must show love: your immediate family members, such as your spouse and children; your parents, to whom you're commanded to show honor; your extended family; your neighbors, who as we discussed in the last chapter may live in your community, church or work; and other friends. What does "love never fails" mean in the context of *all* these people?

Connecting to Love's Source

Efforts to love people from your own sense of self-sufficiency will exhaust your love reservoir in a short period of time. As those reserves run low, you risk feeling taken for granted and unloved yourself, eventually becoming resentful. On the other hand, when your love comes from God, you remain vigilant to maintaining the source of your love and joy. You get recharged from the Lord and are able to bless others from a love that overflows, rather than from your limited reserves.

Here is the key takeaway—the manifestation of your love to your spouse and others will never exceed the source of that love. I appreciate the way theologian Ray Stedman captures the idea of agape love in saying, "This is God's kind of love in which the origin lies not in the one loved but in the one who loves. God loves because He is love; we are to love, because we are of God!"[1]

They have learned to transform their love for one another into something that transcends themselves.

To understand unending love we must focus on the nature of the One who loves. If we want to understand God's love, we must understand His nature. If we want to understand our own love, we must comprehend our own nature.

I submit for your consideration that the script for developing a character of unending love is captured by the apostle Paul in his first letter to Timothy, as he puts forth a charge, the goal of which is love "that issues from a pure heart and a good conscience and a sincere faith" (1 Tim. 1:5).

As you think of your love for your spouse, imagine a stool made of three legs: one leg of a pure heart, one leg of a good conscience and one leg of a sincere faith. A pure heart speaks to the need for wholeheartedness. A good conscience captures the need for godly reverence in the decisions that you make, both individually and as a couple. Lastly, sincere faith is the belief that your marriage is a gift from God, designed to shape you into the vessel of honor that God ordained from the beginning of the world.

To reiterate one of the key points in this book, what you believe is paramount. If you believe that your marriage is committed to unending love, you will be right. Likewise, if you believe that your marriage lacks such commitment, you will be right. Your personal belief is what defines the trajectory of your marriage because your attitudes and behaviors will imitate that belief.

If you believe you are committed, you will demonstrate unending love toward your spouse. You will take personal responsibility for doing everything in your power to align your marriage with this belief. If you do not believe, you will always find in your commitment reasons why it's impossible for you to do so. You will blame your spouse and circumstances for the deficits in your marriage.

A term used in psychology is the "fundamental attribution error." In the marriage context, this error occurs when a husband or wife blames the spouse's mistakes on his or her personal character flaws. For example, a wife might believe her husband forgot it was his turn to pick up their daughter from cheerleading practice because he always prioritizes his work over his family.

Yet she believes her own errors are a result of circumstances rather than questionable character. For example, she might believe that she had no other choice but to lash out in anger at her husband because he jeopardized their daughter's safety.

The reality, of course, is always much more complicated because character and circumstance are interconnected. Couples who demonstrate unending love in their marriage have mastered the apostle Peter's instruction in the next step of our feature passage in Second Peter 1:7—to supplement "godliness with brotherly affection, and brotherly affection with love."

These couples have learned to supplement their deep friendship with an abiding belief that their marriage is God's gift to them, believing they must be faithful stewards of their marriage. This belief compels them to develop the character that aligns with God's conviction and to trust God's providence in the midst of their positive and challenging circumstances.

Make Love Personal

Omar and Jéneen Barlow are lovers. You hear that love when they talk about one another as "prince" and "princess." You see that love in their support of each other's gifts and business ventures. You feel that love in their deep smiles and hearty laughter which seem to accompany them wherever they go. I am not sure if they have learned the art of showing loving affection, or if they are just innately gifted in this way.

Without question, however, they have learned to transform their love for one another into something that transcends themselves—a love for their community. The Barlows' enthusiasm for God, marriage, family, ministry, businesses and life is infectious. Omar and Jéneen have fourteen years of marriage under their belt and three young children; watching how their zest for life influences the lives of so many others is remarkable.

Put simply, the Barlow's mission as entrepreneurs and ministers is to empower people to discover their purpose and fulfill their destiny. Their organization, Barlow Enterprises, is a speaking, coaching and consulting company that inspires, educates and equips people to live lives of excellence. But what really sets the Barlows apart is not their acumen for business strategy or personal development. Although they demonstrate excellence in these domains, what places Omar and Jéneen on a plateau with only a few others is their deep regard for the unique story that unfolds with each individual who is blessed to cross their path.

Many influencers and entrepreneurs pedal formulaic products or systems designed to guide others along their life course, but Omar and Jéneen have an uncanny ability to target and customize their services to the unique needs of each individual.

I saw this firsthand in their hands-on approach with my son after he was arrested for theft for the second time. They would have been justified to judge my son for his illegal activities.

They are constantly replenished by the unending love of God that flows through their marriage and onto children.

How could this teenager, who had been raised in the church with a clear sense of right and wrong, be implicated twice for stealing? As his father, I was outraged and found myself emotionally disconnecting from my firstborn child whose behavior made absolutely no sense to me.

Though I loved my son, I struggled to empathize with him in any way—especially after his second infraction.

Thankfully, my son had the opportunity to connect with Omar and Jéneen. They clearly conveyed that his behavior was unacceptable, but they also empathized with him in a way that helped him to see his destiny through a different lens. The Barlows showed love for my son as an individual and restored his walk with God by fostering his gift for dance. When recently asked about the

Barlows' (particularly Jéneen's) impact on him so many years ago, my son's response brought tears to my eyes. As a teenager, he felt rejected by us, his parents, because he wanted to dance rather than follow the more conventional or predictable career path that we had chosen for him.

He was disappointed and somewhat shamed by the feeling that those who cared about him most felt he was losing himself. He felt judged by us, who saw stealing and dance as evidence that he had lost his identity and his way.

In the midst of this identity crisis, the Barlows entered his life through a program aimed at motivating excellence in teenagers. As my son recounts, Jéneen made him feel accepted by allowing him to do what he felt he was born to do—dance. She helped him disentangle the stealing behavior from his passion for dance.

Though he had clearly erred in stealing, Jéneen validated dance as an expression of God in him. Today my son is a dance professional who recently completed a master of fine arts in dance from Ohio State University.

During his tenure as a graduate student, he was hailed by the dance department as one of their most popular instructors. His students regularly share moving testimonies about the impact of his dance classes on their lives.

Though still young, my son is clearly maturing as a leader in his profession. As a parent, I could not be more proud of him or more thankful for the Barlows' unfailing love that looked deeper into him than the surface. What is remarkable, however, is how Omar and Jéneen continue to replicate this tangible demonstration of love.

As the founding CEO and principal of Eastern University Academy Charter School (EUACS) in Philadelphia, Omar engages all of the teenagers with the same individual attention that was shown to my son. The impact of this model is undeniable. While the city of Philadelphia's public school system suffers with an abysmal graduation rate just under 70 percent, Omar's charter school graduated 100 percent of its seniors. All of them were accepted into post-secondary institutions, and many of them received handsome-sized scholarships. How does he do it?

Omar recounts a recent story of a troubled eleventh grade student on EUACS' website: "In the midst of the daily struggle of moving students forward academically, socially and emotionally, an eleventh grade student has retaught me the lesson of never giving up on a student and the importance of upholding the vision in spite of the things that students do that are totally at odds with the vision."[2]

When outlining the steps that he took to reconnect with this student who was teetering on the verge of expulsion, Omar's advice is to first "speak with love."

But, I wanted to know more. What does it mean practically to speak with love? Omar's response speaks volumes: "Make a big deal about small things." For this wayward teen, Omar recounts celebrating small wins that others might dismiss as routine.

For example, when she called to explain why she missed school one day, Omar celebrated her responsible decision to call rather than chastising her for being absent. This teenager knew that someone genuinely cared and expected more of her, and she rose to the level of those expectations.

Omar's "speak with love" philosophy has fostered a culture of caring accountability at his school that is literally transforming families. Just as they did with my son, the Barlows never give up on a child. This is an inspiring story in its own right, yet it fails to paint a full picture of the source or impact of the Barlows' influence. Despite the exhaustion of parenting three young children and running successful businesses, Omar and Jéneen are able to continuously speak with love and invest in a community in need because they are constantly replenished by the unending love of God that flows through their marriage and onto children, school staff, business leaders and church congregants.

The love that you show your spouse will continue into the afterlife.

Because of Omar's tireless commitment to community development, we were not surprised when he was selected as a finalist for the coveted Steve Harvey "Best Community Leader" Neighborhood Award two years in a row.

Speak with Love

We began this chapter by distilling the sacrificial and unfailing significance of agape love—a significance that distinguishes it from every other type of love. As Christians, we can easily grasp, at least conceptually, that the love God the Father shows toward His children is agape love.

Despite being undeserved, Christ's love is shown through His shed blood, which perpetually washes away our iniquities and makes us presentable to God the Father.

Though we are born in sin and shaped in iniquity, we can come into right relationship with God because of the redemptive act carried out by the only person capable of such sacrifice. Simply put, agape love is redemptive—restoring us to a right relationship with God. It is a central tenet of our faith. Unfortunately, too many of us fail to understand that Christ's work also models for us the manner in which we are to be redemptive in our human relationships with one another. Redemptive relationships are those that cover our shortcomings and shape our character even when undeserved. Redemptive relationships connect us back to God who is the source of all love.

As we learn from Omar and Jéneen, redemptive relationships are demonstrations of spoken love, radiating out from our home into our community.

I had an opportunity to listen to Omar deliver an inspiring Sunday sermon on the Christian's call to kingdom living. His message was simple: all of us have a unique role to play in the kingdom.

As I think about this message, I am reminded of the apostle Paul's instruction to the church at Ephesus to speak the truth in love in order to work together as a unified body of Christ. He then affirms that when each of us is working properly, the Christian community "builds itself up in love."

> Rather, speaking the truth in love, we are to grow up in every way into him who is the head, into Christ, from whom the whole body, joined and held together by every joint with which it is equipped, when each part is working properly, makes the body grow so that it builds itself up in love. (Eph. 4:15–16)

Everything around us will pass away except for this one thing—unfailing love. Such love does not exist in a vacuum. It flows from God the Father into our spirit, and is demonstrated first in the relationships that are closest to us. Marriage is designed to be the ultimate human display of Christ's unfailing love for His children. Marriage is to be both self-sacrificing and redemptive. Marriage is a channel to experience the kingdom of God.

Marriage is agape love because it symbolizes Christ's relationship with the church. Neither you nor I deserve the agape love that Christ shows. It is an act of grace. This is the same grace that we are called to extend to our spouse through the seasons of marriage. The beauty of course is that grace, when stirred up, cannot be contained.

It is supernatural. It spills over onto every place your feet step and every person you touch, with a reach that ultimately extends far beyond where your eyes will ever see. Maybe that is why Omar and Jéneen chose the name Grace for their one and only daughter—to consecrate a life with the sufficiency of God's grace.

Paul's simple words say it best—love never ends. The love that you show your spouse will continue into the afterlife when we each have that moment before the Father and are affirmed by those glorious words, "Well done, good and faithful servant. You have been faithful over a little; I will set you over much" (Matt. 25:21).

Love's Grace Card

I commit to walk by your side for a lifetime with an unfailing love that worships God and channels the light of Christ into life's dark places.

12

Surrender It All

As soon as you learn to never give up, you have to learn the power and wisdom of unconditional surrender, and that one doesn't cancel out the other; they just exist as contradictions. The wisdom of it comes as you get older.

—Kris Kristofferson

During my youth, I played the piano for my Dad's church. Though I was never a proficient pianist, I did have some amazing experiences with God when it was just a keyboard, a hymnbook and me. During some of my lonely teenage days, hymns connected me to the Father. When feeling really down, I'd often play and sing the same hymn for thirty minutes—and in difficult times, I'd sometimes cry while doing so.

At that time, I had a reputation for having a tough, and maybe even caustic, exterior. But something about those hymns connected me—a hurting kid—to God.

Of course, that "something" was the Holy Spirit speaking love to me. One of the songs that I played was the classic hymn "I Surrender All" penned by Judson W. Van DeVenter and put to music by Winfield S. Weeden in 1896. Even today, more than thirty years since my piano-playing days, I still feel the emotion of those lyrics. The song's message captivates me even as I pen this book's final chapter.

The journey of faith and marriage is not for the faint of heart. As you have likely gleaned by this point, this journey is a commitment to pursue both God and your spouse with your whole heart. There are no shortcuts to a great marriage because there are no shortcuts to wholeheartedness.

The Christian life and a thriving marriage demand the surrender of anything within us that is not like God. No book, workshop or self-help program can substitute for your personal commitment to surrender.

An Unfair Faith

Hebrews 11 presents us with an amazing cast of biblical heroes and heroines whose actions immortalized them as models of faith. A quick glimpse through this chapter explains why it's been dubbed the "Hall of Faith." Each hero's and heroine's action is attributed to faith.

The passage reads that *by faith* Abel offered an acceptable sacrifice, Enoch was taken up, Noah constructed an ark, Abraham journeyed to a land of promise, Sarah conceived—and the list goes on with Isaac, Jacob, Gideon, Samuel, David and many others. Every one of these acts was fueled by faith.

We know, however, that this faith did not come easily. Faith always comes at a cost. For Abel, it was the cost of his life at the hands of his own brother. For David, the cost was his personal safety when King Saul attempted to impale him with a spear. At a young age, Isaac faced being killed by his own father as a sacrifice. For Noah, the cost was the social ostracism and public humiliation of building an ark for a rainstorm, which was unbelievable to anyone outside his family. Abraham's wife, Sarah, even suffered with the low self-esteem and social stigma associated with barrenness in their Jewish culture.

Without question, all of these faith heroes paid a price, and the price was always what we would call "unfair." Abel did not deserve to die. Neither David nor Isaac was guilty of anything that should have threatened their lives. Sarah did nothing to cause her inability to bear children. We could go through all the heroes and heroines of faith and arrive at a single grand conclusion—none of them deserved the cost that faced them.

Every faith journey, of which marriage is one, experiences peaks and valleys.

Without exception, the cost was always what we would call unfair. Yet, these are but a handful of the unfair accounts of biblical heroes and heroines. Think of your own favorite Bible hero and his or her faith journey. I can assure you that you will observe the same pattern of unfairness.

Of course, every other act of perceived unfairness pales in comparison to the unjust verdict placed upon Jesus Christ by the Roman governor Pontius Pilate. Pilate attempted to exonerate himself by speaking to the unjustness: "You brought me this man as one who was misleading the people. And after examining him before you, behold, I did not find this man guilty of any of your charges against him" (Luke 23:14). Jesus' death was unfair.

The faith journeys of those biblical heroes listed in the Hall of Faith are marked by unfairness. As I think about these and others who have courageously pursued God's will for their lives, I have concluded that every road to the kingdom of God described in Scripture requires both faith and the willingness to pay a price that at face value seems unfair. Is it worth it? Again, the heroes of Scripture guide us.

Abraham and Sarah's faithful decisions culminated in offspring as numerous as the stars. David's faithful pursuit resulted in his designation as "a man after God's own heart," an esteemed warrior, and a revered king.

Jesus Christ's faithful obedience to God the Father redeems our sins and renders us faultless before God. Yes, faithfulness to God's declaration for us is always worth it, even when the path takes us through unfair terrain. The difficulty, of course, is that only in hindsight can we see the full picture. Hence, we must trust God.

Author Brennan Manning, a Catholic priest turned itinerant evangelist, offers a captivating account of such trust in his book *Ruthless Trust: The Ragamuffin's Path to God.*

The book recounts the exchange between ethicist John Kavanaugh and Mother Teresa during Kavanaugh's three months at Mother Teresa's Home of the Dying in Calcutta, India. Manning writes the following about Kavanaugh's initial meeting with the venerated nun.

> On the first morning there he met Mother Teresa. She asked, "And what can I do for you?" Kavanaugh asked her to pray for him. "What do you want me to pray for?" she asked. He voiced the request that he had borne thousands of miles from the United States: "Pray that I have clarity." She said firmly, "No, I will not do that." When he asked her why, she said, "Clarity is the last thing you are clinging to and must let go of." When Kavanaugh commented that she always seemed to have the clarity he longed for, she

> laughed and said, "I have never had clarity; what I have always had is trust. So I will pray that you trust God."[1]

The secret to an unfair faith is to trust in God rather than in what we perceive. Yes, God encourages us to make wise use of our senses and sensibilities. The ultimate wisdom, however, is yielding to the Holy Spirit's direction. We must obediently surrender all and trust that God's ways are far above our own (see Isa. 55:8–9).

An Unfair Marriage

What must we surrender in order for our marriage to please God? This Christian journey from faith to love is a commitment to surrender our will for God's way, our pride for God's promise and even our life for God's love. This commitment makes sense to us when things are going our way in the marriage and when the connection with our spouse is on the upswing.

Marriage can seem like child's play when romance is in the air and spouses lament over long periods apart. The truth, however, is that marriage is not lived on the mountaintop. Every faith journey, of which marriage is one, experiences peaks and valleys. The presence of God that you felt during your last peak experience must sustain you through the next valley.

When things are strained (e.g., during the dissolution of a first marriage for Clint and Penny, the cancer scare of Wesley and Rose Marie, or the death of a nine-year-old due to bone cancer as with Jack and Judy), we find it difficult to grasp what God is doing. We can feel alone and overwhelmed.

Remember those DRAGONS? Yes, it is hard to understand God's method of allowing adversity to shape us into His image. It runs counter to our human nature. The sacrifice feels so unfair, especially when our spouse takes us for granted, abuses our kindness, wounds us when we are vulnerable or chooses to be unfaithful. We are right to deem this sacrifice unfair. Unfair is precisely what it is.

The message, however, is that unfairness is not your dismay. As the story of Ian and Larissa Murphy showed us, unfairness is your hope, your advantage—but only when it begins with faith.

When these graces are increasing in your marriage, you have an undeniable advantage over the Adversary.

An Unfair Burden

Faith. This was my best word of comfort to give to Johnny and Donna Wyche just a few weeks prior to penning this chapter, when their son Johnny was tragically killed in a car accident.

At twenty-one, he was a fine young man who I considered a mentee. He was heading into his senior year at my undergraduate alma mater, Howard University, where he was on scholarship. I enjoyed interacting with him about school and life whenever he was back home during school breaks.

He was actively involved in church and was loved by many. His future seemed bright in every way. I had talked to Johnny just two weeks before his accident to tell him we had a birthday gift for him. That was the last time I spoke to him before that fateful day.

His death is still so fresh and still feels so unfair. How can he be gone? I don't pretend to be able to identify with the grief that his parents must feel. As someone who has not gone through this type of trauma, I cannot imagine such a loss or the strain it places on a marriage. And the loss seems so unfair for a couple that has been fighting to improve their marriage. Things seemed to be on the upswing in their relationship. Then the phone rang.

We talk about an unfair advantage. Admittedly, on the surface it feels difficult to embrace the notion of an advantage for spouses who feel their marriage has been dealt an unfair hand, whether it's the untimely loss of a child or less painful events. My wife and I are committed to be there for Johnny and Donna for the long haul, whatever it takes.

How can we help this couple grow toward God even through this difficult time? What will it take for them, as a couple, to transform what feels so unfair right now into a God-honoring testimony?

I believe that our feature passage offers them and other marriages a path to a new normal that blesses everyone in their path. As this couple so valiantly affirms in conversations with us and others, their faith serves as their foundation and gives them the courage to move forward through the pain. Without question their eldest son's death dealt a blow to their foundation, but their belief in Divine Provision remains unwavering.

My continued prayer for Johnny and Donna is that they allow the Holy Spirit to guide them through each leg of the journey featured in our central passage.

As I think about the Wyches, other couples and my own marriage, I offer a prayer to God for an unfair advantage.

An Unfair Prayer

Dear God, help us to add virtue to our faith, such that even in the midst of a sense of loss, we can discover a place of wholeness from committing the time and courage to truthful communication through the pains and joys.

Teach us to add knowledge to our virtue, so that we will embrace mutual consideration of our respective needs in healing from the hurts and using these experiences to encourage others.

Help us to augment our knowledge with self-control by finding our own place of contentment rather than despair and conflict.

But guide our understanding that a contented attitude only emerges from a daily decision to pursue Your best for us, for such is the nature of perseverance.

We realize that some days will be easier than others. But through it all, strengthen us to demonstrate godliness that complements our perseverance as we maintain a reverential posture toward You as both the author and finisher of our faith, rather than harboring bitterness or anger.

Give me the sensitivity to be the friend that my wife/husband has prayed for and needs. And convict us to give that friendship liberally to others.

Finally, help us embrace a mutual love that never fails because it is rooted in Your eternal truth.

This is our prayer for an unfair advantage where faith serves as the compass that always points us back to You rather than to what we feel.

This is our prayer. Amen.

Unfair Promises

Throughout this book, I have focused on three verses to capture the graces that complement faith to make your marriage thrive.

Before I conclude the book, however, I want to discuss the next three verses that seal the message of an unfair advantage.

Promise 1: Productivity

After considering all seven of the graces that complement faith, the apostle Peter focuses on their benefits. He writes in Second Peter 1:8, "For if these qualities are yours and are increasing, they keep you from being ineffective or unfruitful in the knowledge of our Lord Jesus Christ."

We will never fall when we commit to increased grace in our Christian walk.

As I dissect this verse, I am so encouraged by its promise. It starts with a conditional statement, challenging me to consider whether or not these graces are indeed increasing in my life and my marriage. God desires to see growth, not perfection, in our spiritual walk and our marriage.

Remember, the two are inseparable. There is no growth in your spirituality that is distinct from your marriage. There is no growth in your marriage that is not an intricate part of your spiritual walk.

Growth is a sign of commitment and resilience to prioritize what God declares your marriage to be over what sometimes feels like an insurmountable obstacle. Growth shows a determination to push your faith over your fears.

But, far too often, we Christians suffer from the same stunted growth that Paul identifies when he tells the Corinthian church that he must address them as infants in Christ because of their spiritual immaturity. "I fed you with milk, not solid food, for you were not ready for it. And even now you are not yet ready" (1 Cor. 3:2).

I must then ask myself, "How much more virtue, knowledge and perseverance have I developed in my faith?" I must ask myself if my marriage can handle solid food. Marital maturity is not about some abstract, spiritual threshold or specific faith level. Scripture challenges us to consider the extent to which the seven graces are increasing in our faith. Are we moving in the right direction and growing closer to God?

This question is important because to live these faith-based graces is to safeguard against ineffective and unproductive living. So, what does this mean for your marriage? In his 1989 national best seller *The 7 Habits of Highly Effective People,* Stephen Covey gained acclaim by enumerating the practices that distinguish highly successful people.[2]

Similarly, Scripture offers us seven graces (virtue, knowledge, self-control, perseverance, godliness, mutual affection and love) that characterize highly effective and growth-minded marriages.

In other words, when these graces are increasing in your marriage, you have an undeniable advantage over the Adversary, because your relationship is grounded in knowledge and trust of God's plan for your life. Without these graces, your life and marriage are ineffective and unfruitful—and it gets worse.

Promise 2: Vision

The next verse gives us insight into the ineffective marriage. Second Peter 1:9 reads, "For whoever lacks these qualities is so nearsighted that he is blind, having forgotten that he was cleansed from his former sins." If these graces are not increasing in our lives, we are blind and lack long-term perspective.

The same is true if our marriages lack commitment to these grace-filled pursuits. A graceless marriage is stuck in a fixed mindset and is blind to God's design. A blind marriage fails to grow because it is human-centered rather than God-centered, short-term focused rather than long-term focused and rule-driven rather than relationship-driven.

This lack of vision occurs as a result of a memory lapse, forgetting that Christ's death gives us the liberty to live gracefully and abundantly.

Promise 3: Never-Ending

The choice is yours. Will your marriage be grace-filled and effective or graceless and blind? My prayer is that you choose grace. In doing so, you confirm your kingdom calling and ensure your marital growth. The benefits of a grace-filled faith and marriage are ultimately captured in the next words of the apostle Peter in Second Peter 1:10: "Therefore, brothers, be all the more diligent to confirm your calling and election, for if you practice these qualities you will never fall."

Scripture shows us that a grace-filled faith is the key to effectiveness and productivity, and the benefits are even more remarkable. A grace-filled faith is fail-proof. We will never fall when we commit to increased grace in our Christian walk.

Similarly, as the collective graces increase in our marriages, they too will never fall. Our commitment to Christian maturity is driven by a grace that guarantees that our marriages will triumph over the DRAGONS who oppose them. Grace is our advantage for fail-proof marriages.

I am grateful to the eight exemplars of grace-inspired marriage that have guided us through this journey to an active faith. Here are eight tips that they strive to practice daily to live out their unfair advantage:

- Kiss each other in a meaningful way every day. (Jack and Judy)
- Pray together each day. (Clint and Penny)
- Infuse fun into the process of working together. (Omar and Jéneen)
- Focus on the real enemy of your marriage. (Albert and Debbie)
- Expect tomorrow to bring a fresh perspective to today's problem. (Johnny and Donna)
- Worship the Lord together constantly. (Chris and Juanita)
- Embrace the Holy Spirit as an intimate ally to discern God's best for your marriage. (Wesley and Rose Marie)
- Obey God regardless of how you feel. (Ken and Charmian)

An Unfair Grace

The benefits of grace are unparalleled, but we must never lose sight of the fact that grace always comes with sacrifice—modeled for us by Christ Himself. Such sacrifice is always an offering to God.

We release relationships that detract us from God's purpose. We abandon comfort and convenience for growth. We wean ourselves from self-interests and replace them with Christlikeness. Christ died for us so that we might die for Him.

These are not just words for Christians to idly recite. Instead, think of them as an act of obedience that influences every facet of our lives. As your redeemer and mine, Christ asks that we give our lives to Him as an acceptable offering. God intends that your marriage, family, work and every other area of your existence point back to Him.

Like the heroes enshrined in Hebrews' Hall of Faith, your life in general, and your marriage in particular, are designed to leave a timeless legacy for one primary purpose—connecting people to God's plan for their lives. God desires that each of us demonstrate obedience worthy of the Hall of Faith described in Hebrews. We have what it takes.

Our biblical heroes and the exemplary couples we have followed throughout this book are models for us not because they did everything right, but because they decided to trust God.

A surrendering Christian marriage is a daily decision to freely surrender all to Jesus out of love for Him.

King David committed adultery. Gideon doubted God's call. Sarah laughed at His promise. Yet in spite of their adversities and shortcomings, each of these faith heroes committed themselves to exercise their faith even when the odds seemed stacked against them.

Your marriage hasn't been perfect. You've fallen short of God's ideal as a spouse. We all have. The beauty, however, is that the trajectory of your marriage is determined only by your ability to hear and trust God's leading, especially when it feels impossible or unfair.

Unfairness, whether experienced between you and your spouse or from external forces, has a way of building your trust in God, because it fosters humility and dependence on the Lord as your advocate. Unfairness breaks down notions of self-sufficiency and merit. Unfairness destroys pretense and shows your strength of character and conviction. Unfairness, despite the difficulty it presents to our situation, is often a bridge to connect us to God's grand plan for our lives.

One thing bears clarification—God never treats us unfairly. The apostle Paul poses a rhetorical question in Romans 9:14: "Is there injustice on God's part?" He quickly retorts, "By no means!" Paul continues in verse 17, "For this very purpose I have raised you up, that I might show my power in you, and that my name might be proclaimed in all the earth" (an Old Testament Scripture found in Exodus 9:16). The message is clear.

The negative situations that occur in your life and marriage are opportunities for God's power to be manifested—drawing us closer to the kingdom of God.

As we conclude this book, my prayer is that its pages have shown you how a devout Christian walk benefits your marriage in ways that bend your own human understanding. This book's message is about a grace-inspired faith that is personally and relationally transformative—in your marriage and beyond.

A grace-filled faith is your unfair advantage because it tests your convictions and shapes your character. A grace-laden faith is actively supplemented with the seven graces that make your life and marriage more effective and productive. How is that for an unfair advantage?

Still, there is more. A grace-based faith also assures you that you will never fall, an unfair advantage that extends to your most vital human relationship—your marriage. But even that is not the full promise of Scripture.

Second Peter 1:11, the final verse in our focus passage, makes the ultimate goal of grace-filled faith and marriage starkly clear.

Peter records it as follows: "For in this way there will be richly provided for you an entrance into the eternal kingdom of our Lord and Savior Jesus Christ."

Your pursuit of a thriving marriage full of faith and grace is one of the measures by which God will one day say to you, "Well done, good and faithful servant. You have been faithful over a little; I will set you over much. Enter into the joy of your master" (Matt. 25:21).

More than any other words communicated in this book, our final passage demonstrates that full measure of your unfair advantage. It is a process of sanctification that grows you and your spouse closer to the people that God called you to be before the foundation of the world. A grace-based faith transforms your marriage into a testimony of the power of redemption on earth and into eternity. This growth-minded marriage influences a world in need of godly role models.

Ian Murphy, our hero of chapter 1 who suffered a brain injury, had to receive special permission by the courts before he was allowed to marry Larissa.

However, the consenting judge's heart-warming words to this couple may best describe the point of this entire book in saying, "You two exemplify what love is all about. I believe that marriage will not only benefit you both but our community, and hope that everyone in this city could see your love for one another."[3] Such is the power and influence of love that never fails.

This chapter started with a simple hymn, "I Surrender All," as a transcendent message of relinquishing within ourselves all that is not like Christ.

I would like to conclude with the lyrics from the first verse of this classic song.

All to Jesus, I surrender;
All to Him I freely give;
I will ever love and trust Him,
In His presence daily live.[4]

As I said before, but want to reiterate: There are no shortcuts to a great marriage because there are no shortcuts to wholeheartedness. The Christian life and a thriving marriage demand the surrender of anything within us that is not like God.

No book, workshop or self-help program can substitute for a personal commitment to surrender. A surrendering Christian will discover the truth of A.B. Simpson's words, "He can make the weakest things in you the strongest, the worst things in you the occasions for the grace which will magnify in you the best and divinest qualities of the Christian life."[5]

A surrendering Christian marriage is a daily decision to freely surrender all to Jesus out of love for Him, a decision to live with trust even in the absence of clarity, as Mother Teresa prayed for John Kavanaugh.

A grace-filled marriage is your unfair advantage because it demands that you daily embrace the freedom, wonder and worship that is only experienced in Christ's presence. Pray for me—that my life and marriage will reflect the words that so deeply stirred my heart all those years ago at a piano in a small Virginia town.

I surrender all for a marriage with an unfair advantage. I will pray for your surrender as well. It seems only fitting to end this book with the words that conclude the whole of Scripture: "The grace of the Lord Jesus be with all. Amen" (Rev. 22:21).

Notes

Chapter 1: A Tale of Two Marriages

1. "Happily Ever After? Not Really, Many Wives Say," *Woman's Day* (June 24, 2009), http://www.today.com/id/31377503/ns/today-today_style/t/happily-ever-after-not-really-many-wives-say/ - .VkLBTK6rSV5.
2. *Marriage Beyond the Vows* is a weekly radio program which airs on Praise 103.9/WPPZ-FM, Philadelphia.–Ed.
3. A.B. Simpson, *A Larger Christian Life* (Harrisburg: Christian Publications, 1998), 182.
4. Larissa Murphy, "Why We Got Married," desiringGod, May 9, 2012, accessed November 10, 2015, http://www.desiringgod.org/articles/why-we-got-married.
5. Ibid.
6. John Piper, *This Momentary Marriage: A Parable of Permanence* (Wheaton: Crossway, 2012), 178.
7. "Couple who wed despite all odds after groom's debilitating accident make touching video of their incredible love story," Daily Mail.com, October 29, 2013, accessed November 2015, http://www.dailymail.co.uk/news/article-2479013/Couple-wed-despite-odds-grooms-debilitating-accident-make-touching-video-incredible-love-story.html.

Chapter 2: Membership Has Its Privileges

1. "New Marriage and Divorce Statistics Released," research release in "Family & Kids," Barna, March 31, 2008, accessed April 2016, https://www.barna.org/barna-update/family-kids/42-new-marriage-and-divorce-statistics-released#.Vw-63XpcBdy.
2. Carol S. Dweck, *Mindset: The New Psychology of Success* (New York: Random House, 2007), 7.
3. Andy Stanley, *The Principle of the Path: How to Get from Where You Are to Where You Want to Be* (Nashville: Thomas Nelson, 2011), 44.
4. Simpson, *A Larger Christian Life*, 101.
5. Shaunti Feldhahn, *Surprising Secrets of Highly Happy Marriages: The Little Things That Make a Big Difference* (Colorado Springs: Multnomah Books, 2013), 179.

Chapter 3: Grace and the DRAGONS

1. "Narcissistic Personality Disorder, Definition," Mayo Clinic, accessed April 2016, http://www.mayoclinic.org/diseases-conditions/narcissistic-personality-disorder/basics/definition/con-20025568.
2. Rick Warren, "*Developing Biblical Self Control?", May 21, 2014, http://www.rickwarren.org/devotional/English/developing-biblical-self-control.*
3. Sendhil Mullainathan and Eldar Shafir, *Scarcity: Why Having Too Little Means So Much* (New York: Times Books, 2013, 13-14.
4. Brené Brown, *The Gifts of Imperfection: Let Go of Who You Think You're Supposed to Be and Embrace Who You Are* (Center City, MN: Hazelden Publishing, 2010), 158.

5. *The Grace Card*, directed by David G. Evans (GraceWorks Pictures, 2010), film.

Chapter 4: Pursue an Active Faith

1. Richard J. Krejcir, "Statistics on Pastors," Into Thy Word, accessed November 11, 2015, http://www.intothyword.org/apps/articles/?articleid=36562.

Chapter 5: Invest in Virtue

1. C.S. Lewis, *The Screwtape Letters* (HarperOne: New York, 2015), 161.
2. Chris Gissentaner and Juanita Gissentaner, *Spouse-ology: Developing and Nurturing an Intimate Marriage* (CreateSpace, 2014).

Chapter 6: Empower Knowledge

1. Brian M. D'Onofrio et al., "A Genetically Informed Study of the Intergenerational Transmission of Marital Instability," *Journal of Marriage and Family* 69, no. 3 (August 2007): 793-809, https://www.questia.com/library/journal/1P3-1314096051/a-genetically-informed-study-of-the-intergenerational.
2. Emerson Eggerichs, *Love & Respect: The Love She Most Desires, The Respect He Desperately Needs* (Nashville: Thomas Nelson, 2004), 324.
3. Gary Rosberg and Barbara Rosberg, *The 5 Love Needs of Men and Women* (Carol Stream, IL: Tyndale House, 2001).
4. Gary Chapman, *The 5 Love Languages: The Secret to Love That Lasts* (Chicago: Moody Publishers, 2014).

Chapter 7: Negotiate Self-Control

1. *Merriam-Webster Online*, s.v. "contentment," accessed May 2016, http://www.merriam-webster.com/dictionary/contentment.
2. Institute for American Values and National Center on African American Marriages and Parenting, study results presented at the National Summit on Marriage, Parenting and Families, (Hampton University, Hampton, VA, September 29-30 2009), http://www.hamptonu.edu/ncaamp/docs/National_Summit_Media_Report.pdf.
3. Jerry Bridges, *Holiness Day by Day: Transformational Thoughts for Your Spiritual Journey*, comp. Thomas Womack (Colorado Springs: NavPress, 2010), 336.

Chapter 8: Commit to Persevere

1. Rose M. Kreider and Renee Ellis, "Number, Timing, and Duration of Marriages and Divorces: 2009," *Current Population Reports*, P70-125 (U.S. Census Bureau, Washington DC: May 2011), accessed February 6, 2016, https://www.census.gov/prod/2011pubs/p70-125.pdf.
2. Matthew Schimkowitz, "How Long Does an Average Marriage Last Around the World?" *Hopes & Fears*, June 4, 2015, http://www.hopesandfears.com/hopes/city/city_index/ 214133-city-index-marriage-lengths.
3. *Dictionary.com*, s.v. "perseverance," accessed May 10, 2016, http://www.dictionary.com/browse/perseverance?s=t.
4. Ibid.

Chapter 9: Embrace a Godly Lifestyle

1. *Matthew Henry Commentary on the Whole Bible* (Complete), s.v. "2 Peter 1," accessed November 11, 2015, http://www.

biblestudytools.com/commentaries/matthew-henry-complete/2-peter/1.html.
2. Ray C. Stedman, "Commentary on 2 Peter: Chapter One," Ray Stedman.org, accessed November 22, 2015, http://www.raystedman.org/2peter/2peter1.html.
3. Inverse Ministries, accessed May 12, 2016, inverseministries.org.
4. Clint Bragg and Penny A. Bragg, *Marriage on the Mend: Healing Your Relationship After Crisis, Separation, or Divorce* (Grand Rapids: Kregel Publications, 2015).
5. Ibid.

Chapter 10: Serve with Mutual Affection

1. Kenneth Tan et al., "Committed to Us: Predicting Relationship Closeness Following Nonmarital Romantic Relationship Breakup," *Journal of Social and Personal Relationships* 32 (June 2015): 456–471, doi:10.1177/0265407514536293.
2. John F. Helliwell and Shawn Grover, "How's Life at Home? New Evidence on Marriage and the Set Point for Happiness" (working paper 20794, National Bureau of Economic Research, December 2014), http://www.nber.org/papers/w20794.
3. Thomas H. Maugh II, "Study's Advice to Husbands: Accept Wife's Influence," *Los Angeles Times*, February 21, 1998, accessed November 11, 2015, http://articles.latimes.com/1998/feb/21/news/mn-21412.
4. Cathy Lynn Grossmann, "Americans' Confidence in Religion Hits a New Low," *USA Today*, June 17, 2015, http://www.usatoday.com/story/news/nation/2015/06/17/americans-confidence-religion-poll/28872253/.

5. Reba McEntire, vocal performance of "Love Isn't Love 'til You Give It Away," on *Behind the Scene*, Mercury Records, 1983, album.

Chapter 11: Imitate Unfailing Love

1. Stedman, "Commentary on 2 Peter: Chapter 1."
2. Omar Barlow, "Saving Brittany," *Think Big Blog*, Eastern University Academy Charter School, November 11, 2015, http://www.euacademycs.org/think-big-blog/saving-brittany.

Chapter 12: Surrender It All

1. Brennan Manning, *Ruthless Trust: The Ragamuffin's Path to God* (New York: HarperCollins, 2009), 190.
2. Stephen R. Covey, *The 7 Habits of Highly Effective People: Powerful Lessons in Personal Change* (New York: Simon Schuster, 1990).
3. Murphy, "Why We Got Married."
4. Judson W. Van DeVenter, "I Surrender All," accessed May 2016, http://www.cyberhymnal.org/htm/i/s/isurrend.htm.
5. Simpson, *A Larger Christian Life*, 101.

CLC
PUBLICATIONS
Fort Washington, PA 19034

This book is published by CLC Publications, an outreach of CLC Ministries International. The purpose of CLC is to make evangelical Christian literature available to all nations so that people may come to faith and maturity in the Lord Jesus Christ. We hope this book has been life changing and has enriched your walk with God through the work of the Holy Spirit. If you would like to know more about CLC, we invite you to visit our website:
www.clcusa.org

To know more about the remarkable story of the founding of CLC International we encourage you to read

LEAP OF FAITH

Norman Grubb

Paperback
Size $5^1/_4$ x 8, Pages 248
ISBN: 978-0-87508-650-7
ISBN (*e-book*): 978-1-61958-055-8

THE UNWANTED GIFT

Tom Elliff

In this book, Tom Elliff shares how he and his wife Jeannie came to view their toughest challenge as a gift. Through biblical study and reflection on a personal trial, he demonstrates how to accept that hardships bring life's greatest measure of God's grace and power. Our most painful problems, though unwanted, can truly be gifts..

Hardback
Size 5 x 7, Pages 116
ISBN: 978-1-61958-234-7
ISBN (*e-book*): 978-1-61958-235-4

STOP YOUR COMPLAINING

Ronnie Martin

Stop Your Complaining explores the often-overlooked sin of grumbling and explains how Christians can adopt an attitude of gratitude and humility. Through stories of men and women of the Bible, cultural figures and even the author himself, *Stop Your Complaining* explores the relationship between discontent and gratefulness.

Paperback
Size $5\frac{1}{4}$ x 8, Pages 144
ISBN: 978-1-61958-205-7
ISBN (*e-book*): 978-1-61958-206-4